Routledge Revivals

The Radical Tradition

Originally published in 1978, Richard Gombin's book traces the recurrent attitudes in the history of the European revolutionary movement which have criticized socialist and communist parties for their authoritarian and bureaucratic tendencies, and which have stressed spontaneity and decentralization as the correct basis from which to change society.

From a critique of Marx, through to an examination of Soviet practice under Lenin, Trotsky and Stalin as a factor in the disillusionment of the left with the methods of the Russian Revolution, Gombin's study examines the concepts of 'workers' councils' as they emerged in several countries after the First World War. This comparative study develops the idea of a 'council communism' as opposed to a 'party communism' which, he suggests, is the fundamental concept in the criticism of orthodox Communism from the left.

The Radical Tradition

A Study in Modern Revolutionary Thought

Richard Gombin

Translated by
Rupert Swyer

Routledge
Taylor & Francis Group

First published in 1978
by Methuen & Co. Ltd

This edition first published in 2010 by Routledge
2 Park Square, Milton Park, Abingdon, Oxon, OX14 4RN

Simultaneously published in the USA and Canada
by Routledge
270 Madison Avenue, New York, NY 10016

Routledge is an imprint of the Taylor & Francis Group, an informa business

Publisher's Note
The publisher has gone to great lengths to ensure the quality of this reprint but
points out that some imperfections in the original copies may be apparent.

Disclaimer
The publisher has made every effort to trace copyright holders and welcomes
correspondence from those they have been unable to contact.

ISBN 13: 978-0-415-56808-1 (hbk)
ISBN 13: 978-0-415-57050-3 (pbk)

ISBN 10: 0-415-56808-0 (hbk)
ISBN 10: 0-415-57050-6 (pbk)

The radical tradition

a study in modern revolutionary thought

RICHARD GOMBIN

TRANSLATED BY RUPERT SWYER

Methuen & Co Ltd

First published in 1978 by Methuen and Co Ltd
11 New Fetter Lane, London EC4P 4EE
© 1978 Richard Gombin
Phototypeset in V.I.P. Palatino by
Western Printing Services Ltd, Bristol
and printed in Great Britain
by Richard Clay (The Chaucer Press) Ltd,
Bungay, Suffolk

ISBN 0 416 66150 5 (hardbound)
ISBN 0 416 66160 2 (paperback)

Contents

Introduction: the alternative   1

1 The Soviet state: myths and realities (1917–21)   10
   The three myths and their history   12
   Bolshevism and its 'detractors'   32

2 The radical tradition in Russia   44
   The growth of Russian socialism in the nineteenth century   45
   Marxism and power: an early critique   62

3 Council communism   81
   The First World War and the emergence of new forms of
      workers' struggle   83
   From left-wing radicalism to left-wing communism   92
   Council communism and party communism   103

4 The critique of Marxian reification   119

   Notes and references   126
   Bibliography   140
   Index   147

Introduction: the alternative

All human societies generate an order of one kind or another, but at the same time produce the negation of this order. Opposition to the established order is an historical phenomenon in two ways. Firstly, both in form and content it is the expression of a given era; secondly, it can never be anything but the expression of its era. Consequently, claims to universality or to timelessness merely display a false consciousness that presents the quest for historically limited power in the guise of radicality.

Negation of the social system occurs on many levels, from simple unformulated activity, which breaks down immediate reality, to fully elaborated revolutionary theory, via a range of inter-mediate stages. The shift from pure action to pure thought is barely perceptible, and it is impossible to determine precisely the point at which consciousness of action leads to the formulation of coherent theory.

The kind of radical opposition that challenges the very founda-tions of power structures probably existed even in primitive societies. Vico, in his *Scienza Nuova* (1725), claims to perceive it in his interpretation of ancient myths. Every type of society has had to contend with challenges of this kind, and the old mole has taken a great many shapes and forms in the course of history: heresy, millenarianism, peasant risings, Luddite riots and machine-smashing. The common factor of all these past revolts – apart from their corrosive effect on the established order – was their inability to see themselves as revolutionary phenomena. They were not sufficiently conscious of their historical character. Most frequently their development was determined by some hoped-for bliss in the hereafter rather than concrete changes in the here-and-now. The radicality of the revolutionary movement was already there, but modestly concealed behind a veil of mysticism or religion.

The manifestations gradually gave way to a clearer formulation in the eighteenth and nineteenth centuries, and the overthrow of the existing social order became the principal objective. As a result, politics emerged as a specialized field, concentrating and expressing men's desire for change.

The French Revolution and its ideologists mark the first steps towards unity between political thought and political action, but even so, radical theory remained wrapped in a cocoon of outward appearances. Negation of society may have been less mediatized than in the past, but it was still heavily disguised, and political discourse merely replaced theological discourse (whether deist or pantheist). Certainly men were now equal before the law as well as before their creator, but the idealistic phraseology of the Declaration of the Rights of Man simply concealed the fact that inequality still existed, in a rearranged form. Behind the enunciation of universal ideals (liberty, equality, fraternity, rights of the individual) lurked the protection of utterly material and contingent interests. The capitalist bourgeoisie which hoisted itself to power in the early nineteenth century announced a complete programme of liberation, expressed in terms of ideals. What in fact it then went on to establish was an unlimited freedom to exploit the infant industrial proletariat.

Nineteenth-century socialist systems, and especially Marxism, were already using historical rather than eschatological language. In their demonstrations of the inevitable development of the industrial era, of class society and its miseries, Saint-Simonism, Fourierism and Marxism explored and analysed the potential forces of their age and its forthcoming contradictions.

Like most of his generation, Marx was infatuated with science, and made tremendous efforts to furnish his theory with all the attributes of a scientific system. In this he was closer to Auguste Comte or to Herbert Spencer than he would have cared to admit. For Marx was really the product of positivism, and he was inclined to scientism the moment he tried to hedge his thought about with guarantees of infallibility. In that sense Marxism is a perfect example of scientist ideology, foreshadowing modern technocracy – it shares with Saint-Simonism the honour of being studied by French polytechnicians, English Labour economists and Swedish trade unionists alike.

Not content with claiming to be a scientific theory, however, Marxism seeks to establish itself as *the* scientific theory of social evolution. This ideological imperialism rejects any conceivable critique in advance, demoting revolutionary voluntarism to the role of mere adjunct. The celebrated 'final shove' required to give birth to the new society is relegated to a secondary role as compared with the evolution of the objective conditions categorically laid down and delimited by Marxism. According to Marx, the march of history and the expropriation of the capitalists 'is accomplished by the action of the immanent laws of capitalist production'. The latter 'begets, with the inexorability of a law of Nature, its own negation'.[1] The ineluctability of the historical process means that we can deduce forthcoming events from a set of laws (of which Marx was the discoverer); better, it makes prophecy and forecasting possible, thus providing us with the one and only reading of social reality. It was only natural, therefore, that Marxism should end up by acquiring a corps of official interpreters of dogma, somewhat reminiscent of religion with its prophets, its scholars and its infallible theologians.

Which is not to say that Marxism, insofar as it is an analysis of social reality, is devoid of scientific logic. Marx's approach was scientific in that he studied the society of his time *empirically* (which was a novelty when one thinks of Auguste Comte's metaphysics, then considered to be the last word in bourgeois social science), and especially from an economic standpoint. It was not scientific where he attributed universal or timeless value to his propositions. Engels, with Marx's approval, even wanted to apply the dialectical method to nature as a whole and to turn Marxism into a cosmogony. So we have a new ideology, stated this time in historical and political terms, but which nonetheless seeks to impose itself on men and things *ad aeternitatem*. Here, though, the imposture is no longer justified by religion and its godheads, but by science and its certitudes.

Marx's claims for the scientific character of his system arise out of the nature of his project. For all ideologies tend to hide their particularist essence (the expression of the interests and aspirations of a specific class) beneath a cloak of universal generosity. The mystification lies in making the victims believe they are (or will be) the beneficiaries of the promised liberation.

From the middle of the last century onwards, Marx's thought was increasingly and definitively deformed by economism and determinism. For one thing, the failure of the 1848–49 revolutions in Europe destroyed Marx's confidence in the spontaneous action of the proletariat. His doctrine ceased to relate to the whole of social reality, and he began to concentrate on analysing this reality from an economic viewpoint. Secondly, he came to see social transformations as merely the result of the evolution of the material forces underlying the economic structures, rather than of the autonomous action of workers in conflict with their social environment.

Marx clearly showed the mystifying character of classical political economy, reducing it to its historical dimensions and relating it to the emerging age of (competitive) industrial capitalism. He then went on to explain the functioning of the economic system in terms of economic sociology, inferring from it a projection into the future that is partly true and partly false. He was not mistaken in perceiving a trend towards socialism (large economic units, the attachment of decision-making centres to a central institution, monopolistic markets). But he presents this as ineluctable and positive, arguing that it will bring about the liberation of all those who are exploited and the elimination of classes. But Marx here reverts to ideology, for his analysis fails to mention the real beneficiaries of this evolution, namely the bureaucratic class, which is the product of industrial society, and which is bound to seek to dominate this society. Above all, he confuses the new ruling class with the proletariat. For the latter remains oppressed, even if in new ways.

In the event, the proletariat is simply the auxiliary of this new class in the passage from competitive capitalism to State socialism (or capitalism): from the proletariat, it draws its delegates, its theoreticians and secretaries, while in turn it enriches the ruling class with its own higher bureaucratized strata, which are already cut off from proletarian reality. Above all, the proletariat places its might and its revolutionary potential at the disposal of the bureaucratic class. History is filled with examples of this kind of camouflage (notably in France, between 1792 and 1794), but its true extent became clear in 1848, in Paris, when the democratic bourgeoisie allied with the extra-mural proletariat[2] in February, only to march against it in June alongside the reactionary bourgeoisie.

From the 1850s onwards, Marxist ideology tended to distort social reality, narrowing it down in line with the ambitions of the rising intellectual bourgeoisie. Thus, Marxist critique, as we pointed out earlier, is reduced to a critique of economic reality.

And this is no accident, for all ideologies bear the stamp of the rationality best suited to the interests of the (in this case, future) dominant class. Here, of course, the rationality in question is that of profit and production. Marx accused competitive capitalism not only of reducing the proletariat to a state of misery but of failing to exploit to the full the potential of the existing factors of production. Social revolution, for Marx, was to be a process of rationalization aimed at eliminating all obstacles to the untrammelled develop-ment of production[3] by freeing the factors of production from their institutional strait-jacket (private ownership of the means of pro-duction, competitive markets). This productivist view of the economy is most congenial to the bureaucratic class (managers, politicians, executives, officers, leaders of workers' and socialist organizations), which has everything to gain from the improved organization of industry and wage-labour. One way or another, this bureaucratic class ends up as both boss and beneficiary.

By dressing itself up as an ideology of human emancipation, Marxism managed to get itself accepted as the theory of reality; at first by the sheer force of its arguments and the critical vigour of its concepts; subsequently, more through physical violence and pro-paganda, when Marxism became the official ideology of the Soviet State and of the Communist International. Seen in the light of a century and a half of capitalist evolution, Marxism clearly emerges as the ideology of a class aspiring to political leadership.[4]

II

For the past hundred years the industrial proletariat has been struggling to obtain integration into bourgeois civilization. Today this has been achieved; the proletariat is no longer hanging around the gates of mercantile society, having gradually been absorbed from within. In other words, having made possible the accumula-tion of capital necessary for industrialization (he was after all the principal actor in the process), the worker has finally got his share of the cake. Marxism (and syndicalism) served as the theoretical instrument in this process of integration, enabling the proletariat to devise its strategy for the conquest of the bourgeois stronghold.

Whether in the guise of social democracy, Bolshevism, Maoism, Fidelism, etc., Marxism served as a theoretical tool insofar as the integration of the proletariat into industrial civilization did not conflict with its own project, which is aimed at the establishment of State capitalism. In fact, this project can only be achieved if all individuals are completely integrated in such a way that no one is left outside the compass of the imperatives of the system.

In short, the workers have now effectively entered the system *en masse* in the industrialized countries. The most obvious consequence of this is that the proletarian is no longer merely a producer, but a consumer as well, and that to be the latter is now perhaps his most important function.[5]

As long as the proletariat was held at bay outside the city, its chief ambition was less to destroy than to conquer that city in order to penetrate it and enjoy its fruits. Marxist–Leninist discourse was highly appropriate to the task: 'strategy', 'tactics', 'temporary alliances', 'conquest of power', 'dictatorship of the proletariat' – the language is that of a state of siege. The Marxist's aversion to the anarchist – with the latter's preference for bombs over the impedimenta of the siege-train – is symptomatic of his desire to have nothing whatever to do with what Bakunin called the 'destructive passion'. On the contrary, the Marxist is deeply committed to preserving as much as possible; like an anxious heir, his first concern is to ensure the integrity of his future inheritance, in the hope of taking over a smoothly running productive machine.

III

The advent of mercantile civilization generates a class of proletarians that constitutes both the base and the substratum of this civilization as well as its most natural product. The gathering momentum of industrialization throws fresh strata, whole classes even (peasants, artisans and small shopkeepers) into the ranks of the proletariat. These classes are urbanized, piled wholesale into factories, cut off from their own culture (in the most neutral sense of the term) and reduced to mere survival (that is, to the reproduction of future proletarians and to the minimal maintenance of their own capacity for work, as Ricardo and Marx noted). To this purely physical process must be added spiritual impoverishment and constraint: the bourgeoisie imposes its own scale of values, its rites and its prejudices upon the mass of producers. Indeed, the bourgeoisie maintains its hold upon the proletariat far more by its spiritual power than by force of arms.

But, even though it participated in bourgeois ideology and populated the suburbs around the towns, the proletariat long remained outside bourgeois civilization. It was excluded on a variety of levels, the most visible clearly being the politico-juridical level. For the proletariat had no political being; and when it finally obtained the right to vote and to stand for election, it gave its votes to outsiders: to radical republicans in France, to the Democrats in the United States and the Liberals in England. The proletariat only acquired a leadership of its own shortly before the First World War, which certainly was an advance on the previous situation, even if it meant that the workers simply came under another form of control. But the worker was also deprived of social being, in that his long working days, his living conditions, his family duties and his very poverty prevented him from enjoying genuine social exchange. His exclusion is most spectacular and most crucial, however, in the field of culture: the proletarian is a complete stranger to the world of the bourgeois, since he does not enjoy the conditions of fulfilment afforded by the bourgeois world.

In terms of bourgeois values, the proletarian is a non-being: money after all is principal among these values, and the worker, by definition, is excluded from the sphere of profit. Education comes once the thirst for gain has been satisfied, but the manual worker will seldom get any further than apprenticeship. Finally, the highest sphere of these values contains all those notions we may call 'idealistic' (patriotism, self-sacrifice in the name of a cause, self-cultivation, invention, discovery, etc.) which are extremely important for the established system and which the proletarian, for as long as he remains a member of his class, can neither share in nor make his own.

At the end of this brief balance sheet the proletarian, in the context of classical bourgeois civilization, appears as a one-dimensional being (in a more literal sense than Marcuse employs): he is a producer, and in terms of the predominant conditions of sociality, he is nothing but a producer. As long as he remains exclusively a producer and is deprived of the fruits of his labour, the proletarian can neither realize his own potential nor even acquire another dimension.

For that he must gain access to bourgeois civilization. And that is the real significance of the economic and political struggle which developed along with the process of industrialization. From the setting up of strike funds to the creation of powerful union organizations, from the timid beginnings of a workers' (or labour or social-democrat) party to electoral victories carrying the 'party of the proletariat' to power, all efforts have been directed towards gaining admission to the bourgeois stronghold.

Over the past century or so the proletariat has adopted ruling-class modes of organization, thought and struggle in order to further its integration into the existing structure. The evolution of the capitalist system itself proved a great help in the process. The gradual transformation from a competitive market economy to a monopoly capitalist economy characterized by large units in which the State plays an increasingly active role, means that State planning is now a key component in the mechanism of production, exchange and distribution. As a result, the role of the State is now an integrating one.

In a parallel development, the entire production machine, in its constant quest for new outlets, is progressively turning to the consumer goods sector. The demand for durable and semi-durable goods and for instant consumption is increasing along with the rise in workers' living standards. In countries whose economic infra-structures are broadly established, where demand for producer goods has already reached a certain saturation point and where the colonial market appears increasingly unpredictable, the consumer goods sector has come as a veritable godsend for investors, and is now being 'colonized' in its turn. The so-called consumer societies are precisely those in which the production machine is increasingly adapted to turning out consumer goods, the demand for which moreover is artificially stimulated, manipulated, encouraged and even created out of thin air by authoritarian methods.

The recent solvency, and even more the future spending power, of the proletariat has made it a vital sector in any modern economy. It is expected to soak up a growing output of goods and services, and therefore it is eagerly solicited, flattered, taken into consideration. In addition to its role as producer it has acquired a further dimension – that of consumer. Henceforth nothing is withheld from it and it may (must, rather) consume everything that is consumable, and notably culture which, in an adapted and simplified form, the mass media now dole out in massive helpings.

In short, two kinds of factor have been at work in the integration of the proletariat into commodity civilization: its own worldly struggles on the one hand, and the evolution of the economic system on the other. This process is virtually complete in most developed countries (at least for native workers; immigrant labour, on the contrary, is obliged to fight the battle for integration all over again). Now that he enjoys theoretically unlimited access to commodities, the workers is in a position to reject and negate them.

IV

The task of the current radical theory is to express precisely this negation. It represents a break with all sectorial revolts and half-hearted doctrines. It is born from first-hand experience of social conflicts, but a number of its elements can be traced back to the tradition of anti-authoritarian socialism. This tradition was entirely stamped out by Stalinism, although even in the nineteenth century it was tending to be overshadowed by Marxism's monopoly of oppositional thought. Marxism extracted from the other contemporary socialist systems those analyses which served its own ends. On completing this ideological grafting operation, Marx pronounced the death of the donor as if the graft had utterly drained the donor of substance.

Nevertheless, the alternative to authoritarian ideology is as old as this ideology itself. It emerged as an antidote to all half-way formulae and, from the outset, identified itself with the cause of the utopia of liberation. The great socialist movement born in the first half of the nineteenth century in France impregnated neighbouring and even distant countries with its rationality. Radical thought took root before State socialism and the various authoritarian conceptions of social organization came to be identified with the theory of the proletariat. It emerged at different periods in most European countries and in the United States, and remained a vital force up to the end of the last century, when it was smothered by Marxist-inspired social democracy. All the same, each revolt, each emancipation movement provides it with an occasion to remind us once more of its existence. It played a part in the great autonomous mass movements in Russia (1905–7), Germany (1918–19), England (1918–26), Italy (1920), Spain (1936–7), Hungary (1919, 1956) and France (1936, 1968). Today it seems highly unlikely that radical thought will ever vanish entirely from view. It is solidly established in the so-called affluent societies and is now beginning to pose a challenge in the consciousness of the masses to all those ideologies based on command and obedience.[6] In short, it presents an alternative, playing out its role before history.

1 The Soviet State: myths and realities (1917–21)

The Russian Revolution of 1917 struck a heavy blow at radicality. The advent of a 'socialist' regime throughout the length and breadth of the Russian Empire more or less overwhelmed every other form of revolutionary thought or action.

The prestige of the Bolsheviks was so great that it completely overshadowed all notions of radicality. For they succeeded in imposing their new revolutionary creed and in obtaining the allegiance of millions of workers throughout the world.

By way of historical simplification we may say that Bolshevik dogma maintained its absolute ascendancy for about half a century. In terms of ideas, this corresponds to what is known as Marxism–Leninism, i.e. Marxism as re-interpreted and brought up to date by Lenin and his followers. Politically speaking or, more exactly, in terms of Realpolitik, this dogma was incarnated in the actions and decisions of the leaders of the Soviet Union. It is of little importance that, in the first phases of the Revolution, they made use of the specialized apparatus of the Communist International (or Comintern) or that, in the aftermath of the Second World War, their enormous prestige enabled them to do without this institution. What is important is that they were perceived as spokesmen for world revolutionary consciousness.

This blind confidence was inevitably troubled by a number of rude shocks: the trials of the old Bolsheviks, Khrushchev's revelations at the Twentieth Congress of the Communist Party of the Soviet Union (CPSU) following the so-called de-Stalinization. Yet the edifice remained intact right up to the middle of the 1960s. At that moment a new generation of revolutionaries began to attract attention in Western Europe and North America (and, to a lesser extent, in Latin America): a generation which gave birth to the anti-authoritarian left in Germany, to generalized confrontation in France (with its recurrent outbreaks since May 1968), the various hippy, yippy, freaks and Students for a Democratic Society movements in the United States, not to mention specific groups (women, racial or cultural minorities, homosexuals, etc.). For the last ten years or so, this generation has been stirring up convulsions throughout modern society that have seriously shaken what is conveniently known as Western civilization, its political systems, its social and even its mental structures. It is seeking other frames of reference for its radicality than orthodox communism, which it looks on as being just as bogged down in exploitation and injustice as Western-style capitalism.

The elaboration of a new radical theory inevitably involves the critique of the semi-secular myth the Soviet State has come to represent. While, until now, this critique was confined to the moral sphere (Russian communists were reproached with Stalin, the concentration camps, anti-semitism, stifling dictatorship) or else to economic questions (critics are still waiting for the economic miracle, welfare is greater and more generalized in the United States), from the 1960s on it has turned its attention to the social foundations of the Soviet regime. The results of this global critique were spectacular: in the space of ten years (1965–1974 roughly) communist parties ceased to attract those who aspire to revolution. Conversely, a new bourgeoisie (composed of skilled workers, white-collar workers and middle-rank executives, teachers, journalists and writers, scientific research-workers . . .), attracted by communism's technocratic promises, have slipped quite comfortably into the mould.

On the other hand those who are attracted by the revolutionary phenomenon no longer suffer the pangs of false consciousness as did their fathers, typified by the hesitations of a Sartre or the uncertain meanderings of 'fellow travellers'. Today's radicals, even if not always sure around which political sect they should gather, are uninhibited and unambiguous in their judgment of historical communism. In this respect, the generation of the 1960s and 70s has made a clean break with the past; spontaneously, it has rediscovered a radical tradition which, however much it may have been masked by the image of the 'official' revolution, has never ceased to exist. Our concern here is to retrace this tradition of criticism of Bolshevism, of the Russian Revolution and of the Soviet State: its development will enable us to grasp more fully the expression of a radicality that is not always aware of its own antecedents.

In reality, the origins of this radicality are twofold: anarcho-populism and dissident Marxism. Before discussing them in detail it is worth making use of the recent historical research on the subject to take a look at the three myths which enabled the Soviet upper class to identify its rule with radicality: the soviets, the self-management and the consensus of the working masses.

The three myths and their history

The soviets

The soviets, or councils, occupy a central place in the saga of communism. They represent the necessary link between the Bolsheviks and the masses, the legitimization of their power. The history of the Russian Revolution as told in Soviet textbooks takes place in two phases: the rising of the masses against tsarist oppression, then against Kerensky's bourgeois democracy, engendered a process of radicalization of which the Bolsheviks were both inspirers and spokesmen, preparing the ground for the second phase of the revolution, October 1917.

In other words, the communists perceive an historical and theoretical continuity between the autonomous origins of the councils and the Leninist theory of the State, a view which is held even by the anti-Stalinist Marxist–Leninists.[1]

This misrepresentation of the true course of events was essential in order to paper over the divergences between the masses and Bolshevik policy insofar as the Bolsheviks claimed, and still do claim, to incarnate the dictatorship of the proletariat. It was vital to create harmony between Party and masses. But this version of the history of the Russian Revolution contains a double mystification. On the one hand, there was not *one* type of soviet, but two quite distinct types. The first made its appearance in Russia in 1905, and we find traces of it up to May 1907. These were councils that had arisen spontaneously out of the January–February 1905 strike. We may say that these soviets largely expressed the self-action of the Russian proletariat. Then there were the Russian soviets of 1917, followed by their central European counterparts. In Russia, at least, their emergence was supervised, provoked even, by all those bustling around the revolution in one capacity or another: politicians, trade unionists, journalists, adventurers and demagogues.

The emergence of councils at the beginning of 1905 cannot be isolated from the overall history of the Russian workers' movement. While it is true that their organization was utterly independent of Bolshevik ideology or the Party (and of any other party for that matter)[2], their roots go back to the institution of workers' delegates elected at the time of the first great strikes at the end of the nineteenth century. Paradoxically, the institutionalization of these delegates very frequently corresponded with the wishes of, and even resulted from, the initiatives of employers and police. A police report of 1901 even envisaged the setting up of permanent delegate committees mandated to negotiate with the employer and factory inspector. By this means, it was thought, it would be possible to channel workers' discontent which, if expressed anarchically, was liable to break out in uprisings and revolts. The paradox is only apparent, for it is always easier to nobble a few delegates than to deal with a mass of angry workers.

On the other hand, workers in a firm were obviously not very enthusiastic about those delegates who enjoyed the approval of the boss and the police chief. As a result they preferred to place their trust in clandestine resistance fund officers (these date from around 1870–80 in Russia), and delegates elected spontaneously on the occasion of a strike.

It should be pointed out here that until 1905 delegates, whether official or clandestine, and both permanent and *ad hoc* committees limited themselves to material demands. It was after the Days of February 1917 that slogans became political and, at Petrograd, took on an anti-tsarist colouring. To restore calm, the authorities set up the Shidlovski Commission to look into the causes of the discontent. Workers were invited to take part in the Commission's work, and a special electoral college was established on their behalf. Thus, the idea of central representation for the workers took shape as a result of a government initiative.[3] Although the Shidlovski Commission failed, the idea continued to develop and workers' councils soon emerged, bringing together elected delegates in the factories.[4]

According to a variety of matching accounts, the 1905 soviets arose absolutely spontaneously and were independent of any external 'initiatives'. The popularity of these soviets among the masses derived largely from the absence of political agitators and party representatives in their midst. They expressed the workers' political and economic demands in a situation where trade unions were non-existent and where the parties had little real influence over the masses. In rural areas, the peasant delegate soviets frequently turned out to be neither more nor less than the old village assemblies (*skhod*).[5]

These features of workers' councils persist throughout the period of revolutionary agitation which lasted from 1905 to 1907. The situation was quite different in 1917. Although the February strikes were completely spontaneous (both the Putilov strikes on the 18th and the general strike on the 25th), the councils did not arise directly out of them as they had done twelve years earlier. This time they resulted from the combined efforts of politicians and workers' leaders.

Alongside this, and at the same moment, i.e. between 23 and 27 February 1917, the politicians of the Duma Committee and the members of the Workers' Group sitting on the Central Committee for the War Industries (an employers' and State organization), attempted to organize elections in Petrograd for a Central Soviet. The impetus for this came from the latter group, which installed itself in the Tauride Palace on 27 February and set up a provisional executive committee of the council of workers' delegates, to which committee several socialist leaders and members of parliament attached themselves. It was this committee which called upon workers and soldiers to elect their representatives. This explains why, when the first Provisional Soviet met that very evening, it still contained no factory delegates![6]

As we have seen, the 1917 soviets were neither an entirely spontaneous nor a completely original institution. It would be a mistake to think, however, that they were *imposed* from above: the idea of a central workers' council was in the air, and was widely favoured by workers and soldiers. What had changed was the way the parties now assessed this institution. Seeing in them a spring-board to power, they wooed the councils from all sides, which explains why the intellectuals acquired decisive influence in the Petrograd Soviet and why this Soviet so rapidly lost contact with the masses.[7] Following the October Revolution, all the different tendencies of socialism were favourable to the councils, and this retroactively. But in reality the rapprochement between the Bolsheviks (limiting ourselves to them alone) and the soviets was a laborious process, involving tactical moves that were fully re-examined and constantly amended.

To begin with, in the spring of 1905, the Leninists rejected the soviets out of hand. Between spring and autumn, this hostility changed to mistrust, a mistrust that characterized Bolshevik dealings with all independent proletarian organizations. The Party was even incapable of devising a doctrine capable of gaining unanimous support;[8] at best they paid lip-service to the councils, at worst they heaped abuse on them.[9] Lenin himself was unable to form a coherent judgment: when the Petrograd Soviet acquired a measure of political leadership, the Russian Social Democratic Workers' Party demanded that the Soviet adopt its programme, arguing that the latter was incapable of implementing a politically proletarian line. Even though it emanated from the capital's proletariat, it was being called upon to become a 'technical apparatus' of the Party, and the Party even went so far as to oppose the formation of the Saratov Soviet in November 1905.[10]

Lenin did, however, fully grasp the importance of the soviets from the point of view of revolutionary power. Despite misgivings, he learned the lessons of 1905 and imposed on his Party the task of introducing its authority into the Petrograd Soviet. As early as November 1905 he began laying the foundations for his 1917 strategy; as he himself pointed out, the workers' delegates were essential to a victorious insurrection. But he had no illusions concerning their permanence, for the victorious revolution would necessarily give rise to other bodies, and the councils could even come to be seen as redundant.

The old doubts reappeared in 1917, with Lenin still absent from the scene; Molotov's programme, drawn up on 28 February, did not even mention the soviets. On his arrival in Petrograd, Lenin astonished everyone with his slogan: 'All power to the soviets'. But, from the outset, he had identifed the revolution with the seizing of power by his Party. The slogan he was now propagating with such vehemence was of a purely *tactical* nature. As if additional proof were needed, see the Bolsheviks' sudden volte-face after the events of 3–5 July 1917, organized under their auspices and designed to force the Petrograd Soviet's hand into seizing power. When the latter refused, the Bolsheviks resumed their old hostility to the institution of the soviets, calling them 'puppets, devoid of real power'.[11]

Thereupon, the Bolsheviks changed their line to 'Power to the poor workers and peasants in order to carry out the Party programme'. Nevertheless, it was also proposed to win the councils round from the inside. When the capital's council regained popularity after repulsing Kornilov's attacks, the Bolsheviks returned to their old slogan of 'All power to the soviets', at the end of September. This time, it was for good, especially now that Lenin's partisans had won a majority inside the councils.

Power was seized in the name of the latter: the Party *gave* power to the soviets and thus established its superiority over them. They now served merely to confer legal form on the Party's power.

As early as December 1917, Maxim Gorky was able to write in the newspaper *Novaia Žizn* (no. 195, 7 December 1917) that the revolution was not attributable to the soviets, and that the new republic was not one of councils, but of peoples' commissars. What follows is history: the councils were institutionalized by the July 1918 constitution, which voided them of all content. This was a superfluous precaution insofar as the Bolsheviks already had complete control over them.[12]

If the councils were still an independent expression of the Russian proletariat in the course of 1917, they only were so partially and ephemerally. Contrary to what happened in 1905, they became the scene of factional and partisan in-fighting: they were fought over partly for their historical prestige and partly for their real leading revolutionary role. The Bolsheviks played their hand masterfully in this struggle. They were unequalled as tacticians, but it would be presumptuous and a perversion of the simple historical truth to try to set them up as the defenders of the soviets if one sees in the latter the expression of the struggling masses.

Workers' control and self-management

The history of workers' control in Russia is contained within the period from spring 1917 to spring 1918. The component parts of this year's exploits were to become the basis of a universal myth and to serve as an example to future revolutionaries.

From the viewpoint of radicality, the history of workers' control is especially important, for the assumption of responsibility for production by the producers themselves is the hard core of its programme and its aspirations. Yet, in fact, the subject is obscured by a twofold ambiguity, semantic on the one hand, political on the other. Terminologically, the word 'control' in 'workers' control' gives rise to confusion when it is not clearly distinguished from the word 'self-management' (or 'workers' management'). In this way, the English *workers' control* and the Russian *rabochii kontrol'* can signify both the assumption of responsibility for management by the workers *and* the control of this management, even if its reality does not lie in their hands. For greater clarity, we ought to employ the terms *self-management* or *workers' management* (*rabochii upravlenia* in Russian).

If this ambiguity was not cleared up, at least in Russia, this is because it did itself derive from the political ambiguity surrounding the very essence of power in socialist society.

There can be no doubt that the majority of Bolsheviks were doctrinally opposed to workers' management, a typically federalist and anti-Jacobin institution. Marxist orthodoxy in this domain called for State production linked to a decision-making centre situated at the top of the pyramid. The Bolsheviks made no bones about their advocacy of this conception right up to the eve of the February 1917 revolution, after which they became less open about it. The Mensheviks, on the other hand, never abandoned this orthodoxy and systematically defended the unions (as economic bodies subservient to the political leadership of the Party) as against the representative institutions of the independent power of the workers such as they appeared in Russia.[13]

If, as does the author, one starts from the view that the prime objective of the Bolsheviks was the conquest of power at the summit and that, in order to attain this, they were prepared to adopt tactics (or even a strategy) at variance with their ideological principles, then their attitude towards workers' management seems fairly clear.

Just as Lenin very early on (as early as November 1905) saw in the soviets an institution charged with enormous revolutionary potential, so workers' management and the institutions which expressed it were perceived as a worthy means of furthering the end.

One should not forget that doctrinal lapses were not uncommon within the Bolshevik Party: the most flagrant example of this was their agrarian programme, which Lenin lifted, lock, stock and barrel, from the social revolutionaries. The slogan, 'The land to the peasants', was in blatant contradiction with the Party's programme and Marxist doctrine, which called for the nationalization of all land. The reason why it was so easy to ignore principles was, of course, that in a country whose population was four-fifths peasant, it would have been impossible to carry out a revolution without their support. And so the Bolsheviks turned to the peasants, thereby legitimizing the 'petit-bourgeois' programme of the despised populists.

The Machiavellianism of this compromise was justified, in the eyes of the Bolsheviks, by the observation that the peasant class was not revolutionary in essence, but bourgeois. One could thus make use of it as a temporary ally, turning against it when it had served its purpose. The working class, on the other hand, was represented as the motive force of history: it would have been rather more difficult to compromise over that. Surely any deceit was liable to look like a betrayal of revolutionary goals?

And yet, in 1917, the Russian working class was undeniably

imbued with the idea that justice required that the bosses be driven out of their factories and that the working class take their place. What coherent Marxist, what effective revolutionary would haggle over that kind of demand?

Which is why the Bolsheviks went along with this line, all the more so in that the left social revolutionaries and various brands of anarchist were vigorously propagating it. But, so as not to appear to have betrayed the working class once power had been conquered, the Bolsheviks took refuge in ambiguity. This took several forms: they came out in favour of workers' control without specifying its exact content; they allowed the various currents in the party free (and contradictory) expression on the subject. By following this flexible tactic one may hope to discover a thread of coherence – defined in terms of the social nature of Bolshevik power.

The way one accounts for the attitude of the Bolsheviks toward workers' management and factory committees depends upon whether one looks at the period preceding the 25 October insurrection or the subsequent period.

The factory committees (*fabzavkomii*)[14] emerged in the wake of the January–February 1917 strikes. They mushroomed throughout Russia, taking on the role of workers' representation inside the factory. Their numerical and political importance grew to the point where the Provisional Government was obliged to regulate their existence and their functions.[15] The decree dated 23 April 1917 limited their role to that of the present-day house committee, backed by a trade union chapel: their legal competence covered such questions as the length of working day, wages, disputes and cultural and social problems.

It goes without saying that this limitation was a dead letter: in the revolutionary upheaval of the period, the establishment of the *fabzavkomii* filled a gap and expressed the aspirations of the workers to self-management. This explains why the committees became controlling elements in cases where the employer remained, but took over the management function in those instances where the old management had disappeared.[16]

The role of the committees expanded throughout 1917 as the soviets increasingly lost contact with the mass of workers and stuck to political programmes proclaimed in advance.

The Bolsheviks were naturally interested in these revolutionary bodies and conquered them from within more easily and earlier than in the case of the councils, inasmuch as the *fabzavkomii* were still free of any massive partisan intrusion. But they implanted themselves in the regional (subsequently national) coordinating bodies, which themselves had little influence over the local and factory committees. Thus, at the first conference of the Petrograd factory committees (30 May–5 June 1917), the Bolsheviks already possessed a majority, and the radicality of their slogans competed with those of the revolutionary left. They cunningly called for 'workers' control' in opposition to the Mensheviks and the social revolutionaries, without ever stating very clearly what they meant by it.

The first all-Russian conference of factory committees (17–22 October 1917) confirmed Bolshevik ascendancy still further. Despite a change of tone among certain Leninist delegates hoping to push the trade unions to the fore, Lenin, on the eve of the conquest of power, heightened the revolutionary role of the committees, 'these insurrectional bodies'.[17]

While the conference concluded that workers' control was essential, it did so cautiously and with reference to its own power, stigmatizing moreover the 'control of workers over the factories in which they work'.[18]

It will be observed that the Bolsheviks' slogans prior to the October insurrection contained the same ambiguity as did *State and Revolution*, written by Lenin in August 1917. On the one hand, they have an anarcho-syndicalist colouring, going as far as calling for the destruction of the State in one case and, on the other, entrusting the management of the economy to the masses themselves, organized in factory committees. But in neither case was the commitment total; the sincerity of faith does not exactly burst through. These radical statements were peppered with conditional clauses and safeguards which voided them of all meaning. The tactical need to 'keep one's ear to the groundswell of the masses', in Lenin's own words, did not fully convince militants confident in their own political education, feeling they had nothing further to learn, not even from that most outstanding school – revolutionary agitation.

The second period, beginning on 25 October 1917, was inaugurated still under the influence of this ambiguity, but this was to dissipate gradually. The exercise of power was to make everything clear enough.

The management of production by the workers was one of the goals of the struggle, proclaimed by the Military Revolutionary Committee on 25 October 1917. That same day, the second congress of the soviets (in which the Bolsheviks held the majority) solemnly approved the decision to establish genuine workers' control while specifying, however, that this meant controlling the capitalists and not confiscating their factories.[19]

Shortly afterwards, the draft decree on workers' control, drawn

up by Lenin, was published. Visibly moved by a desire to concili-
ate the masses, Lenin introduced workers' control into all enterprises employing more than five workers. While legalizing a *de
facto* situation he provided for the annulment of decisions taken by
the *fabzavkomy*, the 'congresses and the trade unions' and made the
workers' delegates answerable to the State for the maintenance of
order and discipline within the enterprise.[20]

This plan, which already marked a step backwards by comparison with the existing situation in certain factories, was still further
watered down before being published in its final form on 14
November 1917. In its definitive version, the decree laid down that
factory committees should be subordinate to a local committee on
which would sit representatives of the trade unions; the local
committees themselves would depend upon a hierarchy crowned
by an All-Russian Workers' Control Council. Moreover, as Pankratova notes, this did not imply workers' management such as
the anarchists had called for, but the supervision and control of
production and prices.

So, in mid-November, we find ourselves on the one hand with a
decree which, while legally introducing workers' control, limits it
and clips its wings, and on the other hand with a situation where
numerous factories are already effectively being managed by the
workers themselves or their representatives. Since the insurrection, workers' management has even taken a real leap forward,
which can be accounted for as much by the flight of a good many
employers as by the ambiguous attitude of the new authorities.

The battle for workers' management was therefore not yet
entirely lost, especially since there was a powerful movement in
favour of imposing it, with spokesmen even among the Bolsheviks. Given the existence of this tendency, we are faced with
two possible interpretations of the decree of 14 November.[21] The
first concludes in favour of workers' power at the base; this was
expressed by the Petrograd Central Council of Factory Committees. The other distinguishes between the function of control on
the one hand, and of management and leadership on the other.
The latter function is reserved for the owner or the director of the
enterprise. This was the interpretation given by the All-Russian
Workers' Control Council in which, as we have seen, the trade
unions had already carved out a place for themselves out of all
proportion to their real importance.

The last word came, paradoxically, from the first all-Russian
trade union congress (7–14 January 1918). It should be pointed out
here that, even in the Bolsheviks' view, workers' management was
becoming a practice and an ideology rooted in the working masses

of the large towns and that, rightly or wrongly, the latter expected a great deal from it.[22] Furthermore, spokesmen for the official doctrine of the party, the one approved by Lenin, asked the factory committees to torpedo themselves and to become an integral part of the union structure, entirely in the hands of the Bolsheviks. Despite resistance by the anarcho-syndicalists, the congress voted overwhelmingly for the transformation of factory committees into rank-and-file trade union organizations.

Lozovsky, the future boss of the Russian trade unions, gives the ideological justification for this. Both at the congress in January 1918 and in a pamphlet (*Rabochii kontrol'*) he set out the reasons for his hostility to worker's management. It would introduce 'anarchy into the production process' and would bring about a return to outmoded phases of capitalist production. Along with Lenin, he called for the 'nationalization' of the workers' movement and the regulation of the economy from the top, the centre in fact. To this end he requested the reintroduction of hierarchy into factories, suggesting that the trade unions could serve as guarantors for this.

There was nothing new in this position at the beginning of 1918, except that the Bolsheviks now proclaimed it officially. It was in line with the statist, Jacobin interpretation of Marxist theory of the social democrats; it accorded perfectly with their own aspirations for a strong, centralized power exclusively in their hands. Also, it had never really been completely masked by the hasty slogans – alien to their system – that the Bolsheviks had seen fit to adopt periodically for tactical reasons. Thus, Lenin had never made much of a secret of the fact that he saw workers' control as a 'prelude to nationalizations' or that an accountable administration should exist alongside the factory committees.[23] Furthermore, certain Bolsheviks had already called for the absorption of the factory committees into the trade unions even before the October insurrection.[24]

The trade unions being brandished against the factory committees were only of recent origin in Russia. By contrast, the *fabzavkomy* were heirs to an ancient tradition of delegation, of 'elders' (*starosty*), in short, of legal or clandestine workers' representation, whereas trade union organizations had been stimulated into life by the parties and were, as a result, battlefields in the struggle for influence between Mensheviks and Bolsheviks. At the moment of the conquest of power, the latter found themselves masters of the trade unions, still poorly represented in the factories. The conflict between unions and factory committees is therefore between a largely bureaucratic structure, without any real base, and the direct organs of political and economic struggle of the industrial proletariat.

This unequal match ended to the detriment of workers' management. After the trade union congress in January 1918, and after putting up a feeble resistance, the Central Council of Factory Committees was absorbed by the 'economic committees' of the North (March 1918). With this last bastion of workers' management laid low, all there remained to do was to *nationalize* industry while handling over the management of the nationalized firms to their old owners (decree dated 28 June 1918). Workers' control was thereby definitively subordinated to the soviet (regional or national) of the national economy (*sovnarhoz*). It was now up to workers' control to decide upon output, production norms and labour discipline. As for management, there was a return to individual decision-making, though with the assistance of a management committee, two-thirds of which consisted of members designated by the supreme regional council of the national economy, while the other third was elected by factory workers who were also *enrolled union members*.[25]

Subsequently, the avatars of the Russian workers' movement fell into the clutches of internecine strife between rival bureaucracies: following an attempt to militarize labour (Trotsky ardently defended this measure), a bitter struggle arose between the leaders of the trade union apparatus and their Party counterparts. This is what the Workers' Opposition episode, finally defeated at the Tenth Congress of the CPSU (Bolsheviks) by the central political machine, was all about.[26] One should not be misled by titles: the Workers' Opposition was merely the name of a Bolshevik fraction that happened to wield power in the union apparatus and not of some free opposition emanating from the proletariat. If the latter was still in existence it was manifesting itself at the same moment, but in a very different manner – in revolts in the countryside and in the Kronstadt rising, which the Workers' Opposition delegates hastened to crush on the ice-floes of the Gulf of Finland.

Opposition of the masses to Bolshevik power

The third cardinal myth upon which Marxist–Leninists have constructed their revolutionary hagiography is that concerning the supposedly unanimous support which the rural and urban proletariat accorded its new masters.

All coercive, unjust or harsh measures were reputedly taken by the commissars by virtue of some fictitious consensus of opinion

uniting the workers of the towns with the poor peasants. Every
expulsion, every internecine struggle for power, and every upset
at the summit took place in the name of a proletariat which each
protagonist claimed to represent. In any case, traitors were always
to be found outside the working class, which was supposed to be
massively behind its leaders.

This unanimity was merely a façade. And yet Bolshevik historians have rather tended to neglect the question of collective
opposition to communist power. All that remain available are
scraps of proofs, hints and eye-witness accounts. At all events, it is
not our task here to write the history of this opposition: that would
amount to rewriting the history of the Revolution, and there can be
no doubt whatever that we are now heading towards a complete
revision of the historiographical axioms we have been living on for
the past half-century. Suffice it to mention two phenomena which
occurred in the period 1917–21 and which bear witness to the
distrust, sometimes going as far as open hostility, on the part of
rural and urban workers towards the Bolshevik authorities. The
two cases in point were the 'Makhnovshchina' on the one hand,
and the Kronstadt sailors' rising on the other. The first lasted
throughout this period, while the second marked the close of it. In
many ways March 1921 was a turning point, after which only those
who were both credulous and disciplined could continue to accept
the Bolshevik vision and version of Russian reality.

The Makhnovshchina was the dual history, military and political, of the revolution in the Ukraine. Militarily, under the command of the anarchist, Nestor Makhno, the insurgent army fought
for three years against the pro-German Ukrainian bourgeoisie,
then against Petliura's nationalist bourgeoisie and, finally, against
the White Generals Denikin and Wrangel, all the while skirmish-
ing with the Red Army.

From a strictly military viewpoint, there can be no doubt that the
Ukrainian insurgents saved Greater Russia from a possibly fatal
White invasion. The *Makhnovisty* were a shield against all invaders
heading for the north and the north-west, at a time when the Red
Army was engaged in other battles – against Poland or, previously, against the White Russians arriving from the north, the east
and the west.

But the military aspect of the Makhnovshchina, however important it may have been in saving the Ukraine, is only of secondary
significance so far as we are concerned.[27] For the Makhnovshchina
was also the symbol, if not the best-organized manifestation, of
political resistance to the penetration of Bolshevik authority into
the southern Ukraine. It also provides evidence of the positive

aspects of mass organization in the Ukraine in 1917–21. The extension of Bolshevik sovereignty into this region could only result
from the defeat of the insurgent army on the one hand, and from
the destruction of the institutions of direct democracy set up by the
peasants on the other.

When the October insurrection broke out in Petrograd it aroused
little reaction in Ukraine, where a revolutionary tidal wave had
been sweeping through the country since the days of February.
Because the Treaty of Brest-Litovsk (March 1918) ceded the
Ukraine to the influence of the Central Powers, this region
remained free from Bolshevik penetration up till the end of the
war, in November 1918. For another few months the Bolsheviks
lacked sufficient forces to stand in the way of the development of
the Ukrainian revolution. It was only in the summer of 1919 that
Moscow set about subjecting the Ukraine to its system of government.

For two years, and despite the incessant to-ings and fro-ings of
various armies, despite pillage, war and requisitioning, the peasants under the Ekaterinoslav government (sporadically imitated
by other regions) were to emancipate themselves from the
economic yoke of the great landowners and the kulaks (rich peasants), setting up soviet-style representative bodies constituted on
a non-partisan basis.

Makhno was both the symbol of this movement for local independence and its soul. From the moment he returned from prison
(at the end of March 1917) he tirelessly set about forming peasant
soviets and unions which were administered locally, permitting
no outside interference from the central authorities (Kerensky's
Provisional Government, the Central Ukrainian *Rada*, communist
People's Commissars, not to mention the Austro–Hungarian or
German occupiers). The political role of Makhno and his followers
consisted of encouraging the very lively libertarian tendencies of
the Ukrainian peoples and of permitting them to express themselves through democratic institutions.

The success of this experiment, despite the hostile conditions,
and especially around Gyulai-Polye, Makhno's native village,
gives an idea of the degree to which the Bolshevik graft was not
taking.

On the strength of their slogans – the factory to the workers, the
land to the poor peasants – the communists nevertheless arrived
with a favourable reputation. But as soon as they were in a position
to penetrate into liberated Ukraine, i.e. from autumn 1918 and
throughout 1919, the Bolsheviks opposed the land distributions
which the peasants, assembled in soviets or in local unions, had

already carried out in accordance with the Leninist slogan. Henceforth, the communists sought to gather the peasants into State farms by nationalizing livestock and beet production.

This policy, carried out in an authoritarian manner, was not at all to the liking of peasants who had divided up the land among themselves on a friendly basis and had formed rural communes on their own initiative. In the face of this massive, Greater Russian Jacobin offensive people were naturally tempted to think there had been a change of government: the Bolsheviks (in October 1917) had distributed the land, the communists (a year and a half later) wanted to take it back![28]

By the summer of 1919, this state of affairs was becoming intolerable to a government seeking to extend *its* organization and *its* conception of the revolution to the entire territory. The military agreements with the Makhnovist army were broken and, in June 1919, Trotsky banned the holding of the fourth congress of workers', peasants' and insurgents' delegates which was to have met at Gyulai-Polye.

The insurgent army's riposte was to launch a counter-offensive. With black flags at their head and equipped with a cultural and propaganda section led by Peter Arshinov, the insurgents drove Party and Cheka officials from every town and village through which they passed.

A new push by the White counter-revolutionaries (Denikin and Mamontov) in the course of the summer of 1919 forced the Bolsheviks, whose army was collapsing in the face of the enemy, to make amends to Makhno and to grant him officially an autonomy which he had never in fact yielded. The next few months were to see the flowering of a genuine free republic in southern Ukraine, with peasants and workers applying the decisions voted on by their delegates. It was at this time that the insurgent army reached its peak (at the end of 1919), with some 80,000 men and with heavy equipment.

Then, early in 1920, the Denikin threat was repulsed and the Red Army turned on its erstwhile allies. The struggle between Trotsky's soldiers and the libertarian peasants was to last eight months before a fresh agreement was signed, this time in order to halt General Wrangel, who was advancing from the Black Sea. Following the joint victory over the White General in November 1920, the Bolsheviks immediately resumed their hostility to the Ukrainian partisans, treacherously executing most of the Makhnovist officers, and pursuing Makhno and the remnants of his army across the Ukrainian plain right through to midsummer 1921. In August, Makhno crossed the border into Rumania with a handful of men. He subsequently reached Paris, where he died in poverty in 1935.

No doubt we can also explain the Ukrainian peasants' resistance to communist implantation by the history of this people who never entirely gave up resisting those they looked on as invaders: the Greater Russians. But in the final analysis it was the authoritarian, Jacobin and bureaucratic methods of the People's Commissars that repelled these peasants hungry for freedom. Makhno's rather rudimentary libertarian message penetrated rural areas all the more forcefully in that it coincided with a secular desire for land and for self-administration. Lenin's professional revolutionaries had sensed this enough to draw up an extremely liberal nationalities programme and to promise land to the poor peasants: on this point, at least, the latter were not going to allow themselves to be caught out. They demonstrated their hostility to what they called the 'commissarocracy', thus giving the lie to the myth of the unanimous masses standing four-square behind the Bolshevik government.

The Makhnovshchina was but one example of massive and obstinate opposition to the penetration of communist power. Certainly it was one of the best-known and most determined. But, with the establishment of 'War Communism', one observes a spate of revolts put down with the utmost ferocity: peasants were whipped (as in the days of serfdom), and armed detachments carried out mass executions and extorted grain by force.

These uprisings were not always inspired by the White Guards, as communist propaganda liked to claim. They were not even invariably provoked by requisitioning. The opposition was also political in nature: thus, the congress of peasants, called in March 1920 by the Bolsheviks themselves, protested against what they called the government of the peasants by the workers. In early 1920, according to a Cheka report, the revolt covered twenty-two provinces. By February 1921, the Cheka was announcing 118 centres of rebellion.

The most savage but also the most typical revolt occurred in the province of Tambov and lasted for a whole year (summer 1920 to summer 1921).[29] The peasants, organized into a 'peasant workers' union' (STK), rose against the Bolshevik yoke, the absence of freedom of speech and of the press. The STK programme called for the 'socialization' of land and sought to distinguish itself from both White Guards and Bolsheviks alike. Contrary to government statements, the movement did not arise at the instigation of the social revolutionaries, the latter in fact being opposed to armed revolt at that particular moment. The central committee of the social revolutionaries even forbade its members to take part in it, and those who did participate (such as the popular leader, A. S. Antonov) did so in a personal capacity.

Throughout the Tambov rising, and before the Bolsheviks intervened massively (February 1921), the province was self-administered by locally elected committees. The Bolshevik Party organization, bereft of mass support, fell apart of its own accord. But the Party, its organization and its Cheka was back in February 1921, riding in the regular army's trucks, having been released by the victories in the Crimea (againt Wrangel) and in Poland. Bitter resistance was kept up till July 1921.

The situation was little different in the towns, except that it was harder to organize resistance, especially durable resistance. With strikes forbidden, along with anti-Party gatherings and propaganda, all that has come down to us by way of evidence of popular opposition to the new masters are the vaguest hints and rumours. All the more so because the War Communism period, while forcing the Revolution to close its ranks in the face of the counter-revolution and the external enemy, provided the political leadership with an opportunity of stifling all manifestations of workers' discontent.

In the event it was not to be War Communism that would be only a parenthesis in the history of Russian communism but the NEP (the New Economic Policy, introduced by the Tenth Party Congress, in March 1921), which marks a temporary break with Bolshevism's bureaucratic, centralizing rationality, politically incarnated in the winter of 1917. Stalin knew what he was up to when he dusted off Trotsky's plan for the collectivization of land: he thus not only perpetuated the latter's 'genius' but also the Leninist tradition which consists of presenting socialism as the acceleration of history in terms of production and productivity.[30]

The professional revolutionaries who had come to power in October 1917 were concerned to develop Russia's capitalist potential to the utmost, to carry the country farther and faster along the road than the feeble bourgeoisie.

All concrete measures taken once the Revolution had got over its brief period of anarcho-syndicalist demagogy (from the withering away of the State in *State and Revolution* to the slogans of workers' control and land to the peasants) made necessary by the conquest of power in the first place and afterwards by its retention, these brutally and obstinately incarnate the original project. The same may be said of the centralization of political and economic power, of the return to individual leadership in the army and in industry, and of the introduction of piece-work and Taylorism (as brought up to date by the State economists).

These measures represent the general line, the *average line*, of the Bolshevik project. A variety of tendencies inclined or corrected it in the direction of greater liberalism or severity. The man who drove things to their extreme limits, who was not afraid (with an outspokenness for which his colleagues had neither the courage nor the calibre) to say out loud what many were secretly thinking; the man who, with his curious mixture of fanaticism and a taste for work well done, incarnated all that the worker of the day hated most – that man was Lev Davidovich Trotsky.

This statement will come as a surprise only to those who are unaware of the history of the early years of the Soviet Republic or who have preferred to ignore it. Historical veracity forces us to recognize that, for as long as he held *effective* power (roughly till 1923), Lev Davidovich rather represents the right wing of the Party, although the scale of reference is somewhat arbitrary.[31]

At any rate, in 1919, on the strength of his experience as the architect and leader of the Red Army, he attempted to instil a number of principles shared by military men of the period into the Russian economy. Only, contrary to any consistent military doctrine, Trotsky founded his assertions on Marxist ideology. He stated his principles with disarming frankness: at the height of his glory and power he had no hesitation about hammering a few Marxist 'truths' into an audience made up of union and party delegates.

The road to socialism, he declared, runs through the highest possible degree of statism. Like a lamp which burns brightest just before dying out, the State before disappearing, takes on 'the most ruthless form of government imaginable', one which embraces the lives of all its citizens.[32]

For, in Trotsky's view, population growth was measured in terms of the productivity of man; it would have been unthinkable to construct socialism on the basis of a fall in production. Furthermore, socialist society signified for him 'the organization of workers along new lines, their adaptation to these and their re-education with a view to a constant increase in productivity'.[33]

But this type of organization presupposed forced labour; Trotsky tried to sugar the pill by assuring the worker he was labouring for the State and no longer for some individual. He brushed aside the 'Menshevik' argument that this represented a return to the serfdom of the past by stating that 'under certain conditions, slavery represented progress and led to a rise in production'.[34] And he was convinced that coercive labour in a socialist society would be more productive than the so-called free labour in the bourgeois societies.

In this respect, there can be no ambiguity: for Trotsky, socialism meant 'authoritarian leadership . . . centralized distribution of the labour force . . . the workers' State [considering itself] entitled to send any worker wherever his work may be needed'.[35]

No government coercion, no socialism. But what form was this coercion to take? There, the 'prophet armed', as the late Isaac Deutscher called him, made no bones about going to the heart of the matter: the militarization of labour. For, apart from the army, no other social organization has felt itself entitled to subject citizens quite so utterly, to dominate them so totally as does the proletarian government.[36] Here then was the model, lying ready for use: the army. This implies that whole regiments would be posted to this or that sector of the economy, that production would henceforth be characterized by the introduction of military-style brigades, discipline and obedience.

Once one has accepted the idea of the militarization of labour – not everyone did so at the time – it becomes possible to look upon the entire population as a pool of manpower to be counted, mobilized and utilized. Not only does this ensure the necessary supply of labour but it also serves to eliminate the legendary 'laziness' so typical of the Russian people. For the task of social organization consists precisely of confining laziness within a definite framework, of disciplining and goading man by means and methods which he himself has contrived.[37]

Militarization, which is an 'inevitable method of organizing and disciplining manpower' in the period of transition from capitalism to socialism, implies free use of the war department's machinery for mobilizing the work force, especially in rural areas, where the process will be carried out under the supervision of 'advanced workers'.[38]

To complete the picture, Trotsky proposed to promote the public image of the technical foreman; to introduce (or rather to reintroduce) piece-work and any other system designed to boost output. Taylor's system which, in capitalist society, contributed to the increasing exploitation of workers, did not suffer this disadvantage under socialism. The necessary counterpart of any form of rivalry between workers was to be individual management, of which Lev Davidovich was a determined advocate; he was not in the least impressed with the notion of collegiate management favoured by the trade unions.[39]

To this it should be added that non-work was forbidden in the Trotskyist system. Deserters from the work front were to be

'assembled in disciplinary battalions or else relegated to the concentration camps'.[40]

If Trotsky's proposals for the militarization of labour were not
adopted by the Ninth Congress of the CPSU (29 March–4 April
1920) it was because the left opposition was still too strong. But on
the other hand, individual management, the return of bourgeois
'experts' (*spetzy*) to their former posts, and the relegation of the
unions to a purely educational role (Trotsky had wanted to turn
them into direct instruments of the State in order to increase
production) were all accepted by the same congress. Trotsky's
ideas were nonetheless partially implemented in the *Tsektran*
organization (the body responsible for the running of the rail-
ways), of which he was the first director, and which he ran along
strictly military lines. One need hardly add that workers' management was dealt its death blow, as was the popularity of the Red
Army Chief.[41]

The winter of 1920–21 saw the last act in this unequal struggle
between Party authority and workers' autonomy. Trotsky's
notions of industrial management, of political democracy and of
daily harassment finally bore fruit in the towns as well. He became
the symbol of Bolshevik authoritarianism, as it was he who gave
the most fanatical expression to these ideas. The conduct of the
workers in the large towns bore witness to the fact that the proletariat did not at all see eye to eye with his definition of socialism.
Not by chance was the bloodiest uprising in Soviet history suppressed by the self-same Trotsky.

The Kronstadt revolt was no isolated event. It was one of a series
of strikes and street demonstrations which broke out during the
winter of 1920–21.

In February 1921, these strikes began to spread, notably to
Petrograd, and the sailors' initiative should be seen as an echo of
the workers' strike in the capital, just a few kilometres away from
the island of Kronstadt.[42] But while the Petrograd strikers were
hunted down by the *kursanty* (officer-cadets), the sailors dug
themselves in on their island or else took refuge on their warships
and were thus well-armed to defend themselves.

On 28 February 1921, a resolution was passed on the battleship
Petropavlovsk following the return of emissaries who had witnessed the organized repression of the workers in the capital; this
resolution called for new elections to the soviets with freedom for
electoral propaganda, freedom of speech and freedom of the
press. The resolution also called for the release of political prison-
ers, for the right to cultivate a patch of land or to practise a craft.
But above all it was the political demands (fresh elections to the

soviets with anarchist and left-socialist participation) that turned the central authorities against Kronstadt.

The Bolshevik authorities have constantly tried to present the Kronstadt sailors' uprising as an affair financed and instigated by White Russian émigrés: this version has recently been brought up against available documents emanating from both émigré and Kronstadt sources. It now seems to be well established that the uprising was in no way linked with an insurrection planned by the White Russians but that it represented the most violent phase of a wave of discontent sweeping through the countryside and the large towns at that time.[43]

If one were to illustrate this episode with a single sentence, one might say that the Kronstadt sailors rose in order to defend the slogan 'All power to the soviets', for which they had fought since February 1917 and, in some cases, since February 1905. The erosion of this line had affected them in particular: in March 1918 the Baltic Fleet's Central Committee (*Centrobalt*), an elective body, had been replaced, by decree, with a council of handpicked commissars. Their own soviet was entirely in the hands of Bolshevik officials. The Kronstadt sailors demanded the restoration of the free and popular character of the soviets.

Despite the anarchist or populist colouring of the demands published in the Kronstadt *Izvestia* (which continued to appear throughout the duration of the 'Kronstadt commune'), the ideology expressed therein would seem to be derived directly from the revolutionary traditions of 1905 and 1917. Thus, for example, the sailors came out firmly for workers' management in the factories, for local autonomy, for decentralization; in other words, as Avrich notes, they resumed the demands of traditional Russian libertarian populism.[44] It is no accident, then, that Trotsky should have been the prime target of the mutineers' propaganda: he represented precisely, to the point of caricature, all the old authoritarian institutions the sailors had hoped to abolish once and for all – the strong State, centralism, discipline, dictatorship.

The 'Kronstadt commune' lasted eighteen days (if one takes as its point of departure 28 February, the day the Petropavlovsk resolution was passed). It was drowned in blood. Trotsky took charge of operations, promising the insurgents that he would 'shoot them down like rabbits'.

We know the aspirations and the everyday life of the Kronstadt sailors from the fourteen editions of *Izvestia* (3–16 March 1921). One's chief impression is of their intense hatred for the Bolshevik Party and for its ramifications in the factories and in offices. No. 5 (7 March) ran a banner headline calling for 'All power to the soviets and not to the parties'. This indeed was the hard core of the political demands being put forward by the masses in the winter of 1921. In a last gesture of dispair, Kronstadt repudiated a communism that amounted to no more than 'bureaucracy plus the firing squad'.[45]

With the repression of the Kronstadt rising, a silence fell across Russia that was to be broken only by Stalin's forced collectivization at the end of the 1920s. The principle of authoritarian, statist socialism had prevailed through sheer force. And yet it was to be years before the avatars of the struggle between the masses and the Party would be mentioned in public: Leninist, and subsequently Stalinist mystification triumphed with the aid of the Comintern, all the more easily in that it was aimed at an audience that needed no convincing. Nevertheless, there had been no shortage of warnings well in advance; they had made short shrift of the myth of a socialism firmly rooted in the masses. Above all, this was the work of the anarchists who, before any of the others, had perceived the potential dangers of Bolshevism as implemented in October 1917.

But the anarchist critique, facing its own ideological assumptions, chiefly attacked the statist, authoritarian or even terrorist nature of soviet power. The task of elucidating the nature of this power by means of socio-economic analysis of the new regime was to fall upon the dissident Marxists.

Bolshevism and its 'detractors'

Bolshevism had a good many enemies right from the outset. By 1950 more or less the entire West had, *officially*, set its face against orthodox communism by adopting its cold-war stance.

The first concern of what is generally termed the left was to distinguish itself from the enemies of the Russian Revolution. But at its extremity even the left developed a critique of the Russian Revolution and Soviet State that owed nothing either to partisans of the cold war or to soft-hearted liberals.

This critique did not derive from some *a priori* ideology, as in the case of 'gut' anti-communists, but from the more or less lengthy practice of (or cohabitation with) communism. Chronologically speaking, the anarchists were the first to denounce the image Bolshevism sought to present to the world. They were followed, in the 1920s, by the dissident Marxist–Leninists, who set themselves up in what they called constructive opposition (reconstruction of a 'pure' party or of a new International) but who in reality completed the destruction of Marxist–Leninist communism.

The anarchists

Anarchist testimony is particularly valuable to us since it does not set out to denigrate one system in favour of another; admittedly, a handful of anarchists did subsequently turn into devotees of the 'American way of life', but that concerns individuals, not a system of thought.

The anarchists had already been active in the revolutionary struggle before 1917; many had distinguished themselves in the field of anti-tsarist propaganda, while others preferred political terrorism. Twelve years, fertile in events, discussions and lessons, had intervened between the 1905 revolution – Russian anarchism's baptism of fire – and that of 1917. Twelve years in the course of which anarchists had worked to define their place on the revolutionary scene, to stake out anarchist thought and its field of action in relation to social democracy and to Bolshevism in particular.

There can be no denying that the mistrust was mutual. Lenin and his friends were too deeply imbued with international social democracy's visceral hatred of anarchism, and had been since the end of the nineteenth century. In 1907, for example, the Second International had voted for the exclusion of all the followers of Bakunin and Kropotkin. However, the dispute was already an ancient one, for it goes right back to the First International.[46]

But things were different in Russia. Both social democracy and anarchism, as *movements*, had grown out of the populism of the 1870s and 80s. Neither, in their revolutionary propaganda and agitation, could ignore the fact that populism had left a deep mark on all potential rebels.

True, right from the first 'Iskrist' period (1900–1903), Lenin had tried to foist on Russia a brand of Marxism that was totally void of all populism. Bolsheviks and Mensheviks alike planned to develop a kind of German-style social democracy of Kautskyist inspiration, with SPD organization and rituals serving as models.

Thus, on the eve of February 1917 we find a Bolshevik Party thoroughly cleansed of all 'impurities' arising from the specifically Russian situation. But between February and October 1917 a social revolution occupied the forefront of the stage, with the parties attempting to manipulate events in the immense drama being enacted. Lenin's role by now was to connect up his party to the current passing through the masses. For this he was obliged not to defend but to disparage social-democratic orthodoxy. For the masses were advancing some very ancient demands whose roots are lost in the history of the enslavement of the free peasants first by the boyars and then by the power-hungry tsars – the very same demands that nineteenth-century populism had reformulated and resuscitated and for which it had supplied a theoretical framework. These demands were for land and liberty, for autonomous craft and agricultural collectives, for bread and justice for all.

There was not a peasant or a worker, in that springtime of 1917, to be found calling on the Bolsheviks to seize power or for Lenin and his colleagues to come and sit in the seats of the ministers of Tsar Nicholas II. This much Lenin knew or understood (unlike Stalin, Molotov, Zinoviev and Kamenev, who took as their sole guide the most recent programme of the RSDWP), and it was perhaps this single feature that made him the master strategist on the contemporary Russian political scene.

Lenin had grasped that, in order to achieve power, it would be necessary to rely on the masses, to adopt their aspirations and to amplify them. With this in mind he wrote the highly libertarian *State and Revolution*, and argued for the adoption of workers' management and all power to the soviets. As a result, between March and October 1917 anarchists and Marxists were able to tread the same road, united in struggle for the same objectives: land to the peasants, the factories to the workers and power, at all levels, to the proletariat.

Having fought side by side with them, the anarchists were the privileged and apparently impartial witnesses of Bolshevik deeds and actions. When things began to go wrong for them, around 1917–18, and as they began to be eliminated by the new masters of the police and the army, they made their disillusionment known to the world at large. Unlike the Mensheviks and the left social revolutionaries they had no ties with the Marxist–Leninists; their ideological system turned out to be more extreme in the end, and less prone to compromise.

Hence the utter detachment of the anarchists' critique of Bolshevik reality. They undoubtedly occupied the extreme position on the ideological scale, and this lends particular value to their denunciation of the Soviet State. It might have spared those who cared to listen (and they were extremely rare in the camp of the revolution) many illusions leading to the realm of false consciousness. Their warnings went unheeded at the time, it is true. But they do constitute the link that leads to the new radicality.

Between 1917 and 1923 the anarchists, first the Russians and then foreigners, increasingly spread the news of what was really happening in Soviet Russia by means of meetings and hastily produced pamphlets. They constantly hammered home one simple truth (one which still seems to escape more than one hard-bitten advocate of *coup d'état* techniques), namely that it was

the masses, and the masses alone, that had set the social revolution in motion, and that they had done so before October 1917.
They had seized the land, the mines, the means of production;
meanwhile, the Bolshevik Party, throwing its programme over-
board, had adopted radical slogans with the sole aim of gaining
control over the masses.[47]

Most anarchists were at first taken in by this tactical Machiavellianism. Even if they were not always allies they did not fail to
make known their support of the Bolsheviks, particularly at the
beginning, and this is true of both Russian and foreign anarchists
alike. The most extreme example of this is the Italian anarchists
who, in their great majority, continued enthusiastically to support
the new regime practically right up to the December 1921 Congress! More precisely we should speak of *solidarity* with a revolution under attack from all quarters: the self-same solidarity that
was to wreak such havoc in the ranks of Marxists torn between
their loyalty to the revolutionary cause and Stalin's crimes. We
have to wait until October 1920, the end of the Russo–Polish war,
before *Humanità Nuova* (a libertarian organ) began to speak of the
need to reaffirm the 'libertarian exigencies' of the revolution in
Russia.[48]

And yet, even if they were not exactly plentiful outside Russia,
early warnings had not been lacking. There was the article by
Robert Minor, returned from Russia, who set out his views in
'Bolshevism and the Revolution', published in the *New York World*,
his article being reprinted by the Italian anarchist journal, *Volontà*,
in June 1919. Minor described how the left opposition had been
stifled and the soviets' rule denatured. The same *Volontà* replied
that this was a pack of lies spread by the bourgeoisie. Then there
was Errico Malatesta's letter, printed in *Volontà* in July 1919, re-
minding his readers that Robespierre's dictatorship had prepared
the ground for Napoleon.[49]

The situation was more or less the same in the other major
countries: France, England, the United States. In the last country,
for example, Emma Goldman valiantly defended the Bolsheviks
against all criticism. As early as February 1917 she wrote a pamphlet, *The Truth about the Bolsheviki*, and in the course of 1918 she
claimed that she was deeply shocked by the revelations of Bresh-
kovskaya, the 'little grandmother of the revolution', whom she
suspected of being mentally deranged.[50]

From 1921 on, more and more stories began to arrive to corroborate the earlier rumours. At the Second International Anarchist
Congress (December 1921), held in Berlin, the Russian anarchists –
released from their Muscovite prisons thanks to the intervention of

foreign delegates to the First Congress of the Red International of Trade Unions (Profintern) – arrived to deliver eye-witness accounts. One should add here that 1921 was also the year of Kronstadt and that even the most credulous anarchists ceased all collaboration with the authorities, at last realizing that the celebrated idealism of the Bolsheviks was just a myth.[51]

Henceforth, the libertarians told all, about their own behaviour, about the new regime, about the everyday life of 'liberated' proletarians. Most of them had borne with the Bolsheviks because the latter were prepared to subordinate their theory (Marxist) to anarchist-inspired practice: by calling for the distribution of land, the disappearance of the bourgeois State, by describing political power as temporary. Even the social revolutionaries admitted that Bolshevik practice, on the eve of the Revolution, had been anarchist. Lenin's 'radicalization' (his *April Theses* followed by *State and Revolution*) dissipated lingering doubts and permitted the formation of a common opposition to the Provisional Government.[52]

According to the historian of Russian anarchism, Paul Avrich, the anarchists began to show signs of restiveness as from September 1917, fearing the Bolsheviks might destroy the soviets. In reality, the situation was rather more complex, for the anarchist family was divided into several branches, from the individualists to the ardent advocates of a strong, structured organization. The fact that several libertarian anarchists took an active part in the October insurrection (four anarchists sat on the Military–Revolutionary Committee) and their subsequent collaboration with the new regime (notably in the defence of the Revolution against the White counter-revolutionaries) is evidence of a more complicated situation: one still finds 'official' anarchists even after the period of repression of the anarchists (1918–21).

The situation changed radically after October 1917 insofar as a new State was being constructed, founded upon an authoritarian system. Anarchists visiting revolutionary Russia noted merely that the tradition of authority from above had not disappeared.[53] The soviets, in which so much hope had been placed, had turned out to be 'puppets, void of all substance'. And, for any consistent anarchist, a council system and the dictatorship of the proletariat (in the Bolshevik sense of the term) are two utterly contradictory ideas.[54] The German anarcho-syndicalist Augustin Souchy, in his impressively thorough account, states that the soviets, now virtually elected on a partisan basis, had become forms of power and that it was the Treaty of Brest–Litovsk (March 1918) that had put an end to anarchist hopes. It was then that the Bolshevik Party became the sole party and introduced its system of terror, its confiscations of grain from the peasants, the death penalty and the all-powerful political police.

While it is true that the anarchists had already lost their illusions before this, it was only in the spring and summer of 1918 that they fell victim to systematic repression: imprisonment, closing down of journals, banning of anarchist meetings, shootings. They were consequently in a position to talk from personal experience about the extent of the terror deployed by the new wielders of power.

From allies, the anarchists became official enemies of the regime in spring 1918, and they were forced to adopt a more critical stance towards the authorities. Their opposition consisted mainly in publicizing, inside Russia and abroad, the facts about the new revolutionary regime.

During this period (1917–18) the Russian libertarians were a far from negligible force. Although their organizations numbered only 12,000 or so active members, they reached thousands more sympathizers who were constantly being appealed to and even mobilized by a highly active press whose circulation ran into thousands. Qualitatively speaking – according to an account that can hardly be suspected of being sympathetic – they represented 'the . . . most active party, the most combative, and probably the most popular of the opposition groups [and] seem to be gaining ground in the towns'.[55] Their popularity and the frankness of their criticisms of the new regime were to prove fatal to them.

The Russian anarcho-syndicalists were particularly vigorous in their denunciation of the state of the factory committees in which, as early as August 1917, they had seen the wellspring of a new social order. But wind of these assessments only spread abroad some time later. A French anarchist, on his return from a perilous journey wrote: 'The role of the factory committees elected by the workers, so important in the early phase of the revolution, is now reduced to the following functions: relations between factory workers and the trade union, restaurant supplies, payoc [the legal food ration] supplies, wood for heating, soap and work overalls.'[56] Though this statement refers to a locomotive-parts factory it takes on a more general character, as witnessed by the accounts of other libertarians, all of whom speak of the 'taming' of the *fabzovkomy*, of the dispossession of their power by the State. Whatever the terms employed, all are agreed that the workers did not control industry.[57]

The years 1920 and 1921 saw a succession of accounts. After dealing with those great pillars of the Russian Revolution, the soviets and workers' management, the truth began to emerge about every aspect. Detailed descriptions appeared of the

bureaucracy, the hierarchy of power leading to extreme centralization, police activities (particularly, and already, those of the
Cheka, the political police), the arbitrary tyranny of the most
minor official invested with a little bit of power. All this was spread
and publicized within a circle of libertarians and syndicalists, and
never left that circle. Yet the raw information existed: 'democratic–centralist' procedures were even described in the course of
congresses; those very procedures that were subsequently to
delight generations of communist militants. Warnings were circulated against the 'Red Internationals' which no longer, in 1920,
served any useful purpose other than to shore up Bolshevik power
by hailing decisions taken by the Russian leaders.[58]

The eyes of the so-called revolutionary left in Europe and North
America were riveted on Soviet power, and were fascinated by
it. Passionate attention was paid to the most insignificant commu-
niqué issued by the Council of People's Commissars; factional
struggles and personal rivalries between the principal figures
on the Russian political scene were eagerly commented on.

But this power, in the process of strengthening its position and
securing status in the international political arena, was slowly but
surely sapping the achievements of the social revolution. The
nationalization of the trade unions, following the stifling of the
factory committees, by now seemed a perfectly normal occur-
rence. The anarchists were alone, or virtually so, in pointing out its
enormous importance in terms of the vital interests of the Revolution. They similarly drew attention to the plight of the peasant,
whose real status was gradually deteriorating back towards the
shackles of the old regime.[59]

Finally, it soon emerged from these accounts that not only could
Bolshevik power not be identified with the Revolution, but that it
had become the chief adversary of the Revolution; and the anarchists did not hesitate to draw this conclusion.

The anarchists tended to be a little thin on socio-economic
analysis of the new regime in Russia. In this first phase, the chief
left-wing victims of the Bolsheviks laid bare and described a reality
that was (deliberately or otherwise) completely unknown. True,
certain anarchists did go so far as to speak of a State capitalism
operating to the benefit of the new managerial and bureaucratic
class.[60] But figures, statistics and sociological analyses of society lie
beyond the 'genius' of anarchism: Bakunin may have prophesied
brilliantly about the future evolution of the 'scholarly classes' (of
which Marx was the brilliant ideologist). His analyses nonetheless
stop at the level of generalities (most of which have turned out to
be accurate). The great sociologist was Marx, and his successors

have taken over this function from him inasmuch as anyone with a taste for social analysis cannot help but be attracted to the author of *Capital*.

The dissident Marxists

It fell to those Marxists who had broken with orthodoxy to subject the Bolshevik regime to merciless quantitative and qualitative analysis in order to back up an argument which, without the anarchists, would never have become lodged in militant consciousness.

The dissident Marxists made their appearance at the same time as the foundation of the Soviet State; more particularly, the dispute concerned the assessment of the world revolutionary movement. With the foundation of the Third International (1919), orthodoxy rapidly came to be defined in terms of membership of this organization (which implied acceptance of its line).

The council communists broke with the Comintern in 1920. Other dissidents were to follow: the Bordigists (followers of the Italian leader, Amadeo Bordiga); oppositionists within the official communist parties; ex-communists who had broken with the movement once and for all, etc. Most numerous, as well as most visible on the outskirts of orthodoxy (despite incessant internal doctrinal battles), and presenting the most thoroughgoing theoretical critique of the Soviet State, were the Trotskyists.

Trotskyism is bound through and through to its own origins and to the birth of the movement. This resulted from the exclusion of Trotsky from effective power, which his partisans are agreed in dating from 1923. Far from interpreting this exclusion as the outcome of a struggle for supreme power between Stalin and his followers on the one hand, and Trotsky and his supporters on the other, Trotskyist tradition sees this episode as a *betrayal* of the Russian Revolution and of the Leninist line. Trotsky himself showed the way, fulminating, in the course of his many successive exiles, against what he termed a Bonapartist coup. The parallel with the French Revolution was intended to mean that Stalinism was a counter-revolutionary phenomenon and that he, Trotsky, incarnated the revolutionary purity of Marxism–Leninism. Hence the need to construct a new International, the Fourth, which was to symbolize the true orthodoxy.

It was around 1936 that Trotsky delivered his quasi-definitive analysis of the Soviet State and of its nature. While having *degenerated* from its socialist character, the Russian State had nonetheless not become a capitalist State, for it still preserved the principal conquests of the Revolution: nationalization and planning. Once property was no longer in private hands but in those of the State, the State remained a workers' State. But in view of the Soviet Union's economic backwardness and of its isolation in a hostile, capitalist world, it had become a degenerate workers' State.[61]

This, Trotsky's central thesis, revived an old debate on the subject of the *nature of the Soviet State*: the conflict was already embittered during the lifetime of the leader of the Fourth International (he was assassinated in 1940). For, by rejecting the 'Old Man's' interpretation one was automatically excluded from the Trotskyist movement, which explains why the debate took place on the fringe of the movement.

What was at stake was the attitude to be taken towards the Soviet Union in the event of war, which from 1936 on, appeared likely enough. For Trotskyist militants, this attitude could only be derived from close analysis of the Soviet State. If it was found that its social base was not (or was no longer) proletarian, then it would be difficult to call for the defence of the 'workers' State'.

So the discussion took on fresh life with the approach of the Second World War, fanned by the latest information arriving from the USSR: the great show trials, the concentration camps, Stakhanovism, bureaucratic corruption. A book which attracted the attention of Leninists hostile to Stalin was written by Yvon, a Frenchman who for many years worked in the USSR, first as a worker and then as a manager. Yvon rejects the view that there is merely a bureaucratic *stratum*, as Trotsky's followers claim. There is, he reports, a dominant *class* and an exploited class: State property merely benefits the few. The social function of this new class corresponds to the present degree of development of technology, science and consciousness.[62]

Documents such as Yvon's gave militants much to think about: many of them left Trotskyism proper while continuing to be active around its fringe and developing new theses. This is particularly noticeable in France between 1936 and 1939, and in the United States from 1939 on. Within this microcosm that was the Trotskyist universe (with its more or less avowed satellites) militants began to talk of a 'new class', of a 'neo-bourgeoisie' drawing the USSR towards an evolved capitalism in line with the modern development demands of a great imperialist nation. This new class arose from the fact that the bureaucracy was in possession of the means of production, wielded the power of decision-making and determined the distribution of surplus value.[63]

The battle raged around the concept of the degenerate workers' State up until 1939, although the analysis was developed no further. In 1939, Bruno Rizzi launched a violent attack on the Trotskyist line: the new State, he argued, is not a workers' State because it contains a *bureaucratic class* (civil servants, technicians, soldiers and experts of one kind and another) amounting to fifteen million people and monopolizing forty per cent of production. Rizzi considered this to be an utterly new type of socio-economic regime, *bureaucratic collectivism*, implying a new form of social organization resulting from a considerable development of productive forces. Rizzi's analysis was certainly attractive and, for the period, it went a good deal further in its grasp of Soviet reality than any other undertaking of this type.[64]

But we would have to await the Germano–Soviet pact, Trotsky's death, the victory of the USSR and its imperialist aims in Central Europe and the start of the cold war before the question of the 'degenerate workers' State' could be dealt with once and for all. It was ex-Trotskyists who in 1949 founded the group *Socialisme ou Barbarie* and the journal of the same name, and who resumed the analysis of Soviet society in class terms and developed it most fully.

Socialisme ou Barbarie's argument, which purports to be Marxist, relies entirely upon an examination of the relations of production, their content and their form. The form is juridically defined by the abolition of the private ownership of the means of production and the nationalization of land, industry and trade. It was this 'social' form that led defenders of the USSR and its regime to call it 'socialist'. But if we examine the content of the relations of production, the reality is quite another thing. Here we are dealing with a bureaucratic class (economic, political and cultural managers, experts, military officers, all kinds of administrators) representing fifteen per cent of the population and disposing of over fifty per cent of consumable income, not to mention unquantifiable privileges. This class is not a bourgeoisie in the classic sense of the term, since its members are not owners in their own right. And it is only within this meaning that there can be no *return* to private capitalism as the Trotskyists claim. Yet it possesses all the characteristics of a class: it disposes of the means of production *on a collective basis*, it determines investment, saving and the distribution of income. Planning, in the case of the USSR, is the channel whereby the interests of this class are unambiguously expressed.

On top of this we find, facing the bureaucratic class, a proletariat, as in any capitalism, possessing the same characteristics. It is exploited, it represents the great majority of the nation (eighty-five per cent) and is reduced to the role of simple operative.

The demarcation line between the two classes passes through

the dispossession, the alienation of the (urban and rural) proletariat from the product of its labour – no longer as under classical capitalism, where it was merely the surplus value that was extorted from the proletariat, but through the absence of any power of decision over its own work. More precisely, the frontier runs between those who *decide* and those who *execute* – just as in monopoly capitalist countries, as the theoreticians of *Socialisme ou Barbarie* would put it. Only, in the latter, evolution has not yet come to a halt, the socio-economic regime being halfway between the private capitalism of the pre-1914 era and the *bureaucratic capitalism* of the USSR.

Thus, Soviet socialism emerges as a kind of 'condensed capitalism', a capitalism whose production has been speeded up by a bureaucratic class employing totalitarian methods. The regime in the USSR foreshadows the evolution of monopoly capitalism in the West; it is the horizon for which we are heading. Under bureaucratic capitalism in its final stage a large number of problems still hampering the productive capacity (investment, income distribution, the pace of work) of private or semi-private monopolies are solved quite naturally. The technocratic class directly establishes production norms as well as consumption and investment objectives. It is not fettered by any kind of competitive market, however minimal, nor by arbitrary and unpredictable decisions taken at the level of the individual enterprise. Everything is decided by the Ministry of Planning: the only remaining problem is to carry out the plan, but that is more a matter for the police (whether trade union, political or secret) rather than for the natural laws of economics. One final and not inconsiderable advantage lies in the fact that *ideological* opposition to the regime is quite simply expunged: the press is planned, just like the rest of the economy, intellectuals become 'mental workers' subject to labour discipline, while political opposition is banned. The field is thus left clear for the decisions of the leader (political, trade union, economic or military), with no risk of the decision-making process being disturbed or even modified by such unpredictable phenomena as strikes, changes in parliamentary majorities, exposure of scandals or even critical articles. A good many Western technocrats consciously envisage this eventuality and some even fervently hope for it, though they are not yet prepared to accept it on purely ideological grounds.[65]

By placing the socio-economic regime of the USSR at the end of modern capitalism's road, *Socialisme ou Barbarie*'s theory breaks entirely with the Trotskyist line, making the latter obsolete. Trotsky himself always hesitated to speak of a class and only in fact saw this situation in terms of a bureaucratic layer. He therefore concluded that the USSR stood halfway between capitalism and socialism. In his view a return to capitalism would only be possible in the context of a social counter-revolution (bringing about a revival of private property). Conversely, he held that the passage to socialism from the existing *transition regime* would be possible as the result of a purely political revolution: it was enough, according to him, to restore political power, which had been appropriated by a clique of bureaucrats, to the proletariat and to its Party, of which he, Trotsky, saw himself as the legitimate heir.[66]

But the Trotskyist transition regime rested (and still does for those who continue to hanker after it) on a fiction: namely that the USSR has left capitalism behind it once and for all. By demonstrating that socialism was merely *concentrated* capitalism, *Socialisme ou Barbarie* had, by way of subtle dialectical reasoning, arrived at the same conclusions as a Bakunin or a Machajski. Radicalism came out of this strengthened insofar as a revolutionary ideology was finally demythologized. The critique of the Soviet regime became an integral part of the critique of modern capitalism as a whole.

In order to progress further, however, it is not enough for radicality to rip off the mask of an authoritarian political ideology under cover of a liberating rhetoric. It has yet to confront the philosophy of social liberation, which seeks to formulate the revolutionary equation no longer in terms of the transformation of the world but of changing everyday life.

2 The radical tradition in Russia

Radical thought is inseparable from the history of Russian social-ism for many reasons. It was in Russia that the first socialist revolution broke out, one that saw the expression of a vigorous current of radical revolt. And yet this same revolution gave birth to a government which, while proclaiming its emancipatory mission, stifled every formulation of radicality beneath its pretensions to hegemony.

We tend to view the march towards revolution in Russia in terms of the irresistible rise of Marxist social democracy. In fact, the organized Marxist movement only made its appearance in tsarist Russia in the last decade of the nineteenth century. A rich radical tradition had existed prior to this. But Soviet historiography, or even the curiosity of the general public, has preferred to recall only certain aspects of this tradition: those which tend to fix Marxism in Russian soil and which accord the political philos-ophy of the Soviet State an honourable revolutionary past.

Nineteenth-century Russia was not lacking in currents of thought or revolutionary groups whose Jacobin inspiration would seem to link up, without any apparent break, with Lenin's Bol-shevism. But a far more powerful tradition, one whose roots spread widely throughout the social soil of the Empire, had truly flourished for 'half a century before being overwhelmed and deformed by the rise of ideologies based on power. An inventory of this tradition yields a rich harvest of elements of which the present revolutionary movement appears to be the direct heir.

This is not to say that historians have ignored the existence of Russian populism and pre-populism; several have produced admirable accounts. What interests us here, consequently, is not so much the turning up of new facts or theories as their reinterpretation in the light of the development of radicality, as we look back from the late 1970s.

Seen thus, the Russian revolutionary tradition emerges as something fundamentally different from Marxist–Leninist ideology; in this sense, we may speak of an *alternative* before its time. But, and this is the other side of the coin of its constructive thought, Russian socialism very early, from the 1850s on, developed a critique of Marxist and Jacobin ideologies, the perspicacity and foresight of which has lost nothing of its relevance to this day. This critique is all the more thoroughgoing in that the theoretical writings of the Russian revolutionaries clearly illustrate the relationship between power ideology and the intellectual class demonstrated by Bakunin. For we see that the evolution of the social composition of the Russian revolutionary movement is accompanied by a gradual transformation of the form and content of its ideology. The intelligentsia, starting out as no more than a marginal group, imperceptibly acquired the aspect and dimensions of the core of a power-hungry class; its socialism was consequently to take on an increasingly authoritarian and statist colouring. The evolution culminated in the emergence of social democracy and Leninism – class and ideology were now in perfect harmony.

As we have pointed out, the critique of State socialism was elaborated in advance. The consequences were projected on the basis of existing signs. The birth of organized Marxism in its social-democratic form was almost exactly contemporary with its radical contradiction, leaning heavily on anti-authoritarian tradition, though already witness to the concrete ambitions of the historic leaders. With Machajski we are still at the crossroads where Marxism, anarchism and revolutionary syndicalism meet. The most perceptive critique of the cruder aspects of Leninism as a power ideology came from within the organization.

The growth of Russian socialism in the nineteenth century

What strikes one today about Russian socialism in the first half of the nineteenth century is its modern, even relevant, aspect. And yet, it did not grow out of any Enlightenment philosophy or national movement in the arts and literature – either of which might have served as a cultural background. It arose out of a combination of ideas directly imported from Western Europe and a tradition of very bitter social conflicts reaching back to the beginning of the eighteenth century.

At the start of the last century Russia was still a country with an agrarian economy (despite a certain industrial concentration in the Urals) in which peasants made up some ninety per cent of the population. The nobility and the clergy had a monopoly of access to culture, but the Church was entirely controlled by the Tsar ever since Peter the Great's reforms, while the nobility as a class was bound to the Tsar and his bureaucracy by common interests. Leisured, unproductive and decadent, the nobility was concerned solely to preserve its privileges and to exploit its serfs.

At least that was the case with most of the nobility; under Catherine II the aristocracy had acquired a veneer of French and German culture, and it was considered good breeding to speak French while having no knowledge of Russian. But the seeds of opposition contained within French literature of that age were slow in flowering. Radishchev's *Journey from Saint Petersburg to Moscow*, the first far-reaching criticism of the existing order, only appeared in 1790.[1] But the shock that really stirred aristocratic circles was the Franco-Russian war, and the army's homecoming in 1815. The example learned from the countries traversed lent direction to the desire for change, giving rise to a reform movement among the officer corps and the landed upper aristocracy. The first secret society was formed in 1816, and December 1825 saw the outbreak of the nobles' rebellion, led by Pestel and Rileyev. The Decembrists were still reformists in the full sense of the term, filled with the ideas of the eighteenth-century French Enlightenment and rationalism.

A truly Russian socialism began to emerge in the 1830s and 40s. With a few exceptions, the first generation of revolutionaries was drawn from the ranks of the middle and upper nobility, and had been nurtured on German philosophy and contemporary French socialist thought. Above all, Hegel's philosophy left an indelible mark on these intellectuals now awakening to revolt. Before even the left Hegelians in the West, Russian socialists gave Hegel's system a progressive interpretation, and they were among the first to apply his dialectic and his phenomenology to politics.[2]

An entire generation (Belinsky, Herzen, Ogarev, Bakunin, Granovsky, etc.) derived the framework of its thinking from Hegel and Feuerbach, but it nonetheless looked to the French socialists for its critique of society and its historical analysis. Even in the Young Hegelians' interpretation, Hegelian thought was susceptible to purely idealist use – to the sublimation of discontent in mere idealism. Herzen's and Ogarev's critique became social and revolutionary with the assimilation of Saint-Simonism.[3] At the end of the 1830s and the beginning of the following decade it was the turn of Fourierism to be propagated among this intelligentsia in revolt.[4] Herzen played a central role in the popularization of socialism in Russia; steeped in both Western thought and Russian tradition, he formulated the purest expression of anti-authoritarian socialism to date.

Herzen's great virtue was that he extracted from the utopian socialists (as they were later to be labelled) those elements which still seem to us to have been most valid. Conversely, he rejected all that was religious, mystical or retrograde in Saint-Simon, Fourier or Proudhon. What attracted him to Saint-Simon was the Frenchman's sense of history, of the succession of forms of society and State. He borrowed Saint-Simon's idea that the struggle between the haves and the have-nots, or exploiters and exploited, to use the latter's vocabulary, would surely take the place of the historical struggles of the past.[5] Similarly, Saint-Simon drew Herzen's attention to the situation of the 'poorest and most numerous class' and its likely fate as a result of the development of industrial civilization. Finally, an idea that constantly crops up in Herzen's writings and whose origins are to be sought in the works of Saint-Simon is that of *palingenesis* or social regeneration. He rid this term, however, of the mystical aura conferred on it by its author, and especially by disciples such as Enfantin, who attempted to build a new religion on the foundations of his master's doctrine. For Herzen, it was a question of the total renewal of society after centuries of oppression and injustice. This 'rebirth' would only be obtained through the revolt of those concerned, whose task it was to root out servitude and eliminate it entirely. In short, he was calling upon them to reinvent freedom.

His deep familiarity with all the systems of thought of his time led Herzen, like most of his contemporaries, to reject the communism of his age, from Cabet right through to Marx. By communism he meant any egalitarian doctrine that subjected man to an *a priori* organization imposed on him by authoritarian means, whether Cabet's Icaria, or Louis Blanc's or Karl Marx's State. As opposed to these, socialism was taken to designate doctrines of association, far more attractive to the Russians. Thus, for example, Herzen recognized the validity of Louis Blanc's social classification in terms of bourgeois and proletarian, but rejected his cramped schema for the organization of labour.[6]

Similarly, if Fourierism aroused a great deal of interest in Russia, this was because it stood at the opposite extreme to the mechanistic communism of Cabet or Babeuf. Fourier enjoyed a great vogue during the 1840s as a result of a series of lectures given by Professor Poroshin at the University of Saint Petersburg, and thanks especially to Petrashevsky, who devoted himself to spreading Fourier's doctrines both through the columns of the 'Dictionary of Foreign Words Employed in the Russian Language' (vol. 2 was published in 1846) and in meetings held at his home between 1845 and 1849. Fourierism gained a great many adherents in Russia – in the provinces as well as in Saint Petersburg and Moscow – thanks to the Petrashevsky circle. There was even an (unhappy) attempt at founding a phalanstery in 1847.[7] Neither Herzen nor Petrashevsky accepted Fourierist religiosity or its cosmogony. But Herzen did agree with the Phalansterian's criticism of bourgeois society, of the immorality of the exploitation to which it gives rise; in short, Herzen agreed with his outright moral condemnation of nascent capitalism as it was to be observed in Paris, Lyon or Marseille. Above all, he shared with Fourier a vision of human happiness. Herzen derived his contempt for all formulae that reduce man to the dimension of producer, citizen or subject from Fourier's associative doctrines. He saw in Fourier a constant respect for the individual as a concrete being with desires and passions. And hence the need to provide for the satisfaction and fulfilment of his aspirations, so that he will not be crushed by 'objective law' and the institutions imposed from above and in which he is quartered. This led him to adopt the feminist teachings of the period, both Saint-Simon's 'rehabilitation of the flesh' and Fourier's attack on monogamy; on reading George Sand he immediately approved her call for independence for women.[8]

One last French socialist was to influence Herzen and, through him, the entire Russian socialist movement – Pierre-Joseph Proudhon. Here again, he discriminated between what was stifling and retrograde in the writings of the illustrious Frenchman and his power of negation. He only became familiar with Proudhon's doctrine after he had emigrated, in 1847 – in other words, at a moment when his own socialism was almost fully developed. He nevertheless borrowed Proudhon's critique of the authoritarian State, along with the fundamental notion that the order of society is not external to individuals; that it is not to be found in some institutional framework, but within individuals themselves, and that it is shaped by everyday life.[9] From

Proudhon, also, he took the conception of socialism as the negation of the past and of the existing state of things, from economic
contradictions to the existence of the State itself. He is very severe,
on the other hand, with Proudhon's writings on the patriarchal
family, on the submission of women to men and on peasant
smallholdings. After years of friendly correspondence Herzen
broke with Proudhon when the latter, having drawn steadily
closer to the Empire, condemned the struggle of the Polish democrats for national independence.

Through Herzen, Ogarev and their generation of revolutionaries, an entire system of Western socialism penetrated
Russia, purified of its authoritarian lapses, its fantasies and its
mysticism. The following generation, which prepared the way for
the movement of the 1860s, was itself imbued with this socialism.
First among these was Tchernishevsky who, drawing his inspiration from Saint-Simon, Owen and Fourier, undertook a more
sophisticated and more technical critique of industrial capitalism.
The influence of non-Marxist socialist thought was thus profound
in Russia. And it left traces even after the emergence of social
democracy, for it lies at the origins of all criticisms of authoritarian systems. But borrowings from Western thought represent only part of the Russian radical tradition; for Russia's own
history of social conflict and the intellectual quality and the
sense of freedom of the men who made it, count for a great
deal.

At bottom, these imports from Western culture served merely as
a framework of thought for Russian socialism. The fabric of revolutionary aspiration is embedded in the history of modern Russia,
and in the social conditions of the first half of the nineteenth
century.

From the sixteenth and seventeenth centuries onward, this history is characterized by increasing political centralization, together
with the subjugation of foreign peoples. In the eighteenth century,
the conquest of the surrounding territories to the east and the
south-east was virtually completed, and the Tatars, the
Tshouvashes, the Mordves and the Bashkirs were definitively
annexed to the Empire. But this process did not go unresisted: Slav
peasants rejecting servitude and foreign peoples clinging desperately to their independence rose in revolt, massacring nobles and
officials, and briefly held up the inevitable process of subjugation.
These bloody risings mark Russia's social history over a period of
two centuries, and they still continued to erupt in the mid-
nineteenth century; a semblance of social peace was only established with the abolition of serfdom in 1861.

The plainest result of these revolts was the perpetuation of insubordination and distrust of all forms of external authority and of bureaucracy in any form. On top of this, the foreign peoples managed to preserve a certain degree of independence even when their revolts were most bloodily suppressed. Thus, the various Cossack tribes guarding the eastern and southern borders (particularly against the Turks) received in return a form of local autonomy giving them the illusion that they had not submitted to the central government.[10]

The risings of Stenka Razin and Bolotnikov in the seventeenth century, and of Pugachev in the eighteenth, were merely the most massive and spectacular of an unbroken series of local risings. The Pugachev saga amounted to a veritable social war, in which subject peoples and Slav peasants allied in an attempt to overthrow the Tsarina (Catherine II).[11] But the immediate aim of these numberless revolts was to uproot and abolish the social power of the nobles, the great landowners.

Russia had not experienced the gradual rise of a bourgeoisie accompanied by changes in the social structure (disappearance of the vast estates in favour of peasant smallholdings and medium-sized estates) or in the political structure (evolution towards a constitutional regime), with the result that opposition to the autocracy could not be channelled into institutional outlets. The choice was: submission or revolt. Any challenge to the existing order, therefore, immediately took a radical turn, aiming to destroy the very foundations of authority.

The second tradition on which Russian socialism was nurtured and which to some extent constitutes its hard core is that of the autonomous peasant village – the *mir*. In the *obshchina* (community) each peasant was allocated a parcel of land commensurate with his capacity to cultivate it and with the size of his family. There was a periodic redistribution, and property was owned collectively, not individually. Finally, the *mir* peasant had the impression that he was his own master, or at least that he could appoint his own masters, and especially the *starost*, the elder who filled the role of mayor of the village. Even so, one should not be taken in by the legend (oligarchies very soon established themselves within the *mir* and came to dominate the administration of the community), but still, notions of self-government and collective ownership of property were very deeply ingrained in the Russian peasant mentality. And this perhaps explains why both the political authority of the central government and the social and economic authority of the *baryn* (landlord) appeared to him as illegitimate and a threat to his independence. In extreme cases the Russian peasant even preferred to flee in search of virgin land, out of the reach of officials and soldiers.

It was this historical reality, this secular spirit of insubordination that intellectuals were trying to rationalize in the 1830s and 40s. Although their socialism was expressed in terms borrowed from Western thought, it was nonetheless profoundly indigenous; better, it benefited from the observations and analyses of the French and German philosophers and of English reformers such as Robert Owen, while rejecting all pretence, and anything that contradicted its initial project.

The man who best expressed the principles of a radicality capable of existing in its own right by making use of the terms of Western discourse was undoubtedly Alexander Ivanovich Herzen (1812–70). Herzen was neither a builder of systems nor a constructor of schemas; he produced no doctrine that was entirely new to the Russian thought of his day. There is no such thing as 'Herzenism' in the way there is a 'Marxism', or a 'Fourierism'. Herzen's genius lay in his ability to express the latent ideas of his time; to gather the scattered reflections one could hear in many a Saint Petersburg or Moscow salon, into logical propositions. He was a positive sounding board for socialist ideas in Nicolas I's Russia. A remarkable prose stylist, he even went so far as to forge the political concepts of socialism in his own language, transposing them from the French and the German.[12] Far more than Bakunin (whose ideas only began to penetrate into Russia in the 1870s) he influenced several succeeding generations of revolutionaries, from the 1830s and 40s onward, through his articles in the 'Annals of the Fatherland', and his 'Letters from France and Italy'. Above all, it was through the Free Russian Press, founded in London in 1853, that he was to exercise an immense influence over the Russian intelligentsia, first through the columns of *Polarnaia Zvezda*, and then, from 1857 on, through *Kolokol*, which he edited with his friend Nicolas Ogarev. Herzen's direct influence spread over a quarter of a century, and it remained perceptible in populist thought until the 1917 Revolution.

For Herzen, the principal task of socialism was to construct a world in which human dignity and freedom would be preserved to the greatest possible degree. He insisted on the *dignity* of the individual above all else because it was singularly trampled on in tsarist Russia: there were neither laws nor customs to protect the individual from the arbitrary exercise of authority. The serf was entirely subject to the whims of his master, the noble to those of the tsar and his bureaucracy. In a land where the slightest criticism of the autocracy could earn its author ten years in prison or more, this demand for dignity occupied a central place in all social thought.[13]

These concerns led Herzen to reject all authority imposed from above or from outside the individual, and to place his faith in 'natural groupings'. No *a priori* institution, conceived in advance and in the abstract before being projected on to society, could lead to liberation. On the contrary, man found the conditions for fulfilment in the *mir*, or the *artel* (a kind of artisan community), in other words in voluntarily accepted associations, for it was only in an association of this kind that he could hope to be master of his own fate.

In his concern for man as a concrete being, with real needs and aspirations, Herzen highlighted those aspects of Western social thought that took account of the multi-faceted nature of freedom; beginning with feminism, which he did not distinguish from socialism as such. The revolution was to go way beyond schemas providing for new institutions; for Herzen its goal was the transformation of the very structures of existence.[14] The most important of these were to take place within man's psyche: the humane and rational world he longed for could not be expected to spring forth, fully formed, from the theoretician's imagination. And Herzen, moreover, was sufficiently clear-headed to realize that this kind of socialism was unlikely to emerge in the foreseeable future. However idealistic his doctrine, it cannot be accused of utopianism, and it does not claim to be capable of immediate application. It is presented as a *possibility*, not as a scientific theory.[15] His pessimism towards the end of his life demonstrates the realism that characterized his thought: 'One cannot free men in their external lives if they are not free within themselves.'[16] He concluded that the nineteenth century would not see the birth of men possessing sufficient internal freedom to be able to spread this freedom throughout the social system. His contemporaries were living under despotic, or at best authoritarian regimes, and they were too deeply scarred by servitude to be capable of rebuilding anything other than systems that would oppress the individual. The new society can only be built by a new man, brought up in freedom.[17]

Herzen's doctrine of the State reveals the same realism. He early declared himself in favour of the suppression of central State power and of the institution of federalism and local autonomy.[18] But his negation of the State lacks the absolute and ideological force of Bakunin's views. He had no illusions as to the immediate historical possibilities of abolishing the State in practice.[19] But this in no way detracts from his critique of centralization, of 'external' authority and political power. He remained convinced that federalism alone could guarantee men's freedom; but, he added, it was for men themselves to implement it in practice. In all this he was not projecting abstract schemas into the future:

> . . . A republic that does not lead to socialism seems to us an absurdity; a socialism that tries to dispense with political freedom and equality before the law will rapidly degenerate into authoritarian communism. . . . Republicanism means freedom of conscience, local autonomy, federalism, the inviolability of the individual.[20]

What has dated least in Herzen's thought is precisely the radicality of his goals, made the more credible by his lack of illusion concerning the revolutionary possibilities of his age. Certainly, massive industrialization had not yet begun in his country and there was as yet no urban proletariat, with the result that it is tempting to label his socialism idealistic, tainted with pre-industrial romanticism (which is what E. H. Carr and to some extent M. Malia do). But it was precisely his position as a Russian aristocrat travelling throughout Europe that gave him an advantage over the French or German socialists. For, not having grown up and lived with capitalism, he never accepted its rationale; while Marx (but also Louis Blanc) studied the economy of his age in detail, forecasting its future evolution, thus working within the system and adopting its limits as his own, Herzen himself remained outside industrial capitalism all his life. And that despite the fact that he spent fifteen years in London. . . .

Though a witness of industrial capitalism, he refused to have anything to do with it. Which is not to say that he did not understand it or that its logic escaped him. On the contrary, we have already noted his mastery of the economic critique of Fourier, Saint-Simon and Louis Blanc. Everything aroused his curiosity; he was a voracious reader, and talked incessantly with his great friend Ogarev, who himself took a deep interest in political economy. But it was because he understood Western capitalism that he rejected it, refusing to believe that it could evolve towards liberty. Bourgeois civilization disgusted him: for him it was incarnated in the character of the eighteenth-century Figaro, but a Figaro turned legislator. His conception of freedom was opposed both to the bourgeois world and to bourgeois revolutions. A few months' stay in Paris and Rome (in 1847–8) sufficed to convince him that bourgeois revolution could only transform society into a bourgeois society. Consequently, he stigmatized all ideologies arising out of it, perceiving the oppressive potential contained in them.

In Herzen's view, what characterized bourgeois-inspired ideologies of change was their scientific pretensions. Herzen himself was well-versed in the physical sciences of his age, having studied them at Moscow University, and having pursued them throughout his life. His own doctrine was based on a materialism that nonetheless left some room for conceptualization.[21] But he went on to explore its limits: for him, science was incapable of predicting the future. And he looked upon all teleological theories, even scientific ones, as being of a metaphysical order: narrow determinism mutilates life, and is scandalously indifferent to means and consequences. He also rejected positivism, utilitarianism and pure materialism. The bourgeois revolutions of the nineteenth century seemed to him to have changed little: they conformed to contemporary revolutionary schemas, but they proposed neither to abolish the authority of the State nor to provide the individual with the means to run his own life. From 1848 onwards he was clearly convinced that the destruction of capitalist institutions was not enough – a mentality thousands of years old would have to disappear from our social structures, from the family, private life and relations between individuals.[22]

As a result, we are called upon to place our trust in the creative powers of the masses, in their sense of freedom and in their imaginative potential. We should reject 'closed' systems which, even when they claim to be socialist, perpetuate the religious and authoritarian principles of the old world. All forms of evolutionism are oppressive, since they subject the individual to 'objective law'. For Herzen, the world is governed rather by the possible than by the inevitable, and the future depends upon the active will of men. In short, the revolution must go beyond ideology. Communism, seen as a closed and completed system, was liable to end up as nothing more than 'Russian autocracy stood on its head'.[23] And he went on to write, concerning all the narrow determinisms of his age:

> No, the paths of history are by no means fixed immutably. On the contrary, they change according to circumstances, the understanding and the energy of men. If the human personality is created by the environment and by events, the latter in turn are the product of human personalities, and they bear their stamp: there is reciprocal action between the two.[24]

This open-ended socialism, in search of total revolution, was also shared by many of his contemporaries, starting with Belinsky and Bakunin. It was to be transmitted to the following generations and incorporated in populism; later it was to survive in anarchism. But even in Herzen's lifetime it was watered down, transformed and shaped according to the tastes of the day. This was due to the emergence of a new generation of militants after 1860 whose socialist thought more closely reflected the social composition of the new revolutionary movement. Russian socialism evolved alongside social structures which were themselves in a period of transformation, and in this respect the early 1860s mark an important turning point.

The fundamental principle of radical thought in the 1830s and 40s – of which Herzen was the most talented exponent – and its irreducible core, lies in the notion that only criticism and destruction of the existing world are revolutionary. All constructive principles laid down in advance are liable, as one might say today, to be recuperated by the system.

This is also the most important aspect of the heritage handed on to the following generation, a generation that gave life to and lived through the populism whose foundations had been laid by Herzen, Ogarev and Bakunin. Only, this populism was irremediably and progressively evolving towards Jacobinism and 'organizing' systems. All the principles laid down earlier and all warnings were being swept aside by the rise of a new class, one which seized on socialist thought merely in order to turn it into an ideology in the image of its ambitions. It should be added, whatever may have been said to the contrary, that when Marxism took permanent root in Russia, in the 1890s, its appearance should not be seen as an intrusion. The entire evolution of Russian thought during the twenty years prior to this had prepared the ground for a system capable of taking over where Jacobinism had left off; a system that was superior in the eyes of the intelligentsia in that it now stood completely shorn of the populist elements that had weighed down home-grown socialism.

In order to understand the nature of this evolution it will be necessary to examine the transformation of social structures in Russia right through the nineteenth century. What is most striking in this evolution is the emergence of a class of intellectuals, the intelligentsia, which expressed the revolutionary project right up to its fulfilment in 1917.

Certainly, the intelligentsia as a class was not peculiar to Russia; its existence can be observed in all countries that have undergone capitalist development. But while in the West, in France or in England for example, it remained barely distinguishable from the capitalist bourgeoisie whose privileges it enjoyed, and from which it often originated, in Russia it quickly became a class of its own, for a native bourgeoisie in the economic sense only really arose at the beginning of the twentieth century. The latter had no institutional existence in the first place, as it had no *status* in a society still characterized by a feudal structure;[25] above all, it had no economic existence, since the land, and hence the capital capable of being invested, was in the hands of the nobility. But the latter was utterly unproductive: it lived a life of leisure, or else was in the service of the tsarist bureaucracy, but in any case it saved little. It was still less interested in the prospect of investing in industry or trade. The Urals had had to be industrialized on the orders of the tsar, who forced a number of rich merchants and ironmasters to set up workshops and factories at an indicated spot and to bring in the necessary machines and workers.

So there was no middle class in Russia with the classical entrepreneurial mentality found in Western economies. But the seeds of a middle class did exist, somewhere between the illiterate peasantry and the backward nobility, whose survival and well-being depended upon the transformation of the economy. However, the intelligentsia in Russia had no capital, with the result that it lacked a mercantile mentality – it was unfamiliar with the notions of investment, productivity, unit costs, profits. Its level of education and its professional occupations (government or provincial bureaucracy, tertiary sector), on the other hand, meant that it acquired a technocratic, managerial outlook long before this developed in Western Europe.

The Russian revolutionary movement was largely identified with the mass of the intelligentsia, though its exact composition varied between 1830 and 1890. Between 1825 and 1860 we are dealing with a category made up of nobles and aristocrats even. The universities in any case were practically closed to commoners before Alexander II's reign, and the radical intelligentsia of the 1830s and 40s was drawn from the high landed aristocracy (there were a few exceptions, notably the commoners Belinsky and Nadezhdin). This feature also provides us with the key to the socialism of the first half of the nineteenth century, namely its essentially aristocratic flavour. That is, some of its fundamental characteristics were borrowed from the feudal mentality. It was profoundly radical, and entirely *disinterested*. Seeking neither fortune nor privileges, a Herzen could demand nothing short of the totality. Since he did not seek power, which he despised, he was the natural enemy of all power. Identifying with the immense mass of pariahs, these young aristocrats were hoping that the mass would accede to their level of consciousness at one bound. But above all, their position had made them acutely sensitive to the dangers lurking within all systems of 'plebeian' origin, and with a marvellously prophetic sense they unearthed the hidden ambitions of such systems.

However intransigent, this essentially aristocratic socialism was so above all in the content of its demands. And it can only be described as utopian insofar as it failed to perceive, or at least did so insufficiently, the impossibility of its immediate realization. Herzen, moreover, had no illusions on this point. On the contrary, his intransigence was perfectly justified, as subsequent history was to show, and the present generation of revolutionaries, one that has lived through the affluence of the highly industrialized countries, may very well end up making the Russian pre-Marxist project its own.[26]

On the other hand, this first generation of revolutionaries was anything but dogmatic where means were concerned. Placing their hopes in the autonomous activity of the peasantry (i.e. the immense majority of the oppressed of that period), they had no intention of deliberately stirring up its spontaneity. They perceived the minimal conditions of its true liberation, but they could hardly be said to have drawn up a timetable or an itinerary.

The generation of populists of the 1860s and 70s remained faithful to this programme where its goals were concerned, and its ideals were still the *artel*, federalism, the *obshchina*, the peasant revolution. While thoroughly steeped in Herzen's libertarian demands, the new generation was far more impatient for results. Tchernishevsky's articles in the 'Contemporary' were read avidly, while his 'What is to be Done?' (1863) became the gospel for this generation. Tchernishevsky straddled the two periods: he still admired Fourier and Saint-Simon while carefully studying political economy and applauding Louis Blanc's proposals for the organization of labour. He also thought that Russia could, and should, bypass a phase of bourgeois development, but at the same time he proposed State intervention to aid the establishment of peasants' and workers' cooperatives. Similarly, he was more confident than Herzen in the liberating potential of science.[27]

Already the first 'Zemlia i Volia' (land and liberty), a clandestine organization founded by émigrés in London, but heavily influenced by Tchernishevsky, had raised the question of the need for intellectuals to *guide* the peasant movement (its programme dates from 1861). And the 'Young Russia' group, in its manifesto of the same name (1862), moved rather closer to Jacobinism, and sought to transpose the methods of Barbès on to Russian soil. The content of the projected revolution is still social, but it is taking on a distinctly political form, in the tradition of Robespierre and revolutionary dictatorship.[28]

Nihilism, which in fact was more of an intellectual fashion than a political movement, continued to flourish, accentuating these Jacobin and élitist characteristics after 1863 and the collapse of the hopes raised by attempts at reform. The nihilists were ferociously positivist, swearing by the exact sciences alone while despising everyone not versed in them. For them, salvation would come neither from the people nor from reforms, but only from the educated strata of the population – of which they considered themselves to be the finest products.[29]

The 1860s also saw the first, shortlived, revolutionary groups organized into secret societies and favouring terrorism. Nechaev was a typical representative of these revolutionaries, admirers of the peasantry and its natural organizations while intoxicated with positivism and their own historical role. Nechaev was as influenced by Bakunin as he was by the Babeuf conspiracy; he dreamed of organizing the 'mental proletariat' and of imposing upon it a revolutionary committee whose power would not wither away after the revolution.[30]

But it was Tkachev who was to be the spokesman as well as theoretician of Russian Jacobinism. He made no bones about his belief in economic materialism, and he believed in the superiority of an egalitarian State, which would serve as the true architect of the social revolution. The advent of this State called for the constitution of a political force, as the masses were incapable of casting off their yoke unaided. It fell to the intellectual élite, therefore, to build up this force in the shape of a political party.[31]

Clearly, Tkachev had nothing to learn from Lenin or Trotsky: at least he set forth his project with perfect clarity, without concealing his view that it was for the intelligentsia, and more particularly its most advanced elements, to bring about the revolution in place of the masses.

Nevertheless, Tkachev's objectives and his class analysis show that he was still under the influence of populism: his egalitarian State was conceived as reproducing the autonomy of the *obshchina*. The struggle he envisaged was directed against the nobility, while the beneficiaries were to be the peasants rather than the workers.

All these voluntarist and narrowly political conceptions of the struggle germinated between 1860 and 1870. They resulted in the 'Go to the People' movement and, subsequently, terrorism.[32] 1863 saw the first pilgrimages to the countryside. Hitherto, the revolutionary movement, which had consisted mostly of students, had been entirely cut off from the people. But especially between 1869 and 1873 it was to discover the realities of Russian peasant life when hundreds, or thousands even, of intellectuals flocked to the

villages. Occasionally they settled down to live among the peasants, but most of them returned to their cities disappointed. The
peasant was ignorant, and could not even read the pamphlets the
intellectuals brought with them; what is more, they discovered the
peasant was deeply attached to the tsar and that his only quarrel
was with the nobles. Finally, of course, it was impossible to
attempt the slightest action because of the absolutist police regime;
these migrations were invariably succeeded by massive arrests.

    Revolutionary circles could not fail to draw their own conclu-
sions. Before one could hope to educate the masses and convert
them to socialism it was necessary to create the appropriate political conditions. It was imperative that the struggle be directed
against the State. The doctrine of the second 'Zemlia i Volia'
flowed from this disappointment and the ensuing conclusion: for
adherents it was no longer a question of waiting for the peasants to
carry out their social revolution but to *precede* it. And while the
content of the movement's demands remained populist, this content was already beginning to be overshadowed by the question of
means: centralized organization, stirring up of revolts, planned
terrorism. From 1877–8 onwards propaganda was supplanted by
agitation and bomb outrages, shootings and so forth. In 1878 Vera
Zasulich shot at Trepov, while 1881 saw the assassination of Alexander II.

    One should not get the impression that this evolution took place
without resistance and argument within the revolutionary movement. On the contrary, there was no lack of critics, from Herzen
who accused the young activists of 'Babouvism' and Bakunin who
warned of the positivist dangers stalking the new generation, to
Peter Lavrov, who held that the masses did not wish for a new
government to replace the old one and that the revolution should
come through the rising of 'natural' groupings. Inside Russia itself
there were divergences between those who saw revolution as a
spontaneous phenomenon – as a sort of generalized revolt – and
those who wanted to seize power through conspiracy and to *use*
the State machine in order to bring about social change.[33]

    One way and another, the 'lack of peasant response' hastened
the inexorable march towards organization and 'political work'.
The desire for efficiency was clearly visible among those members
of 'Narodnaia Volia' who favoured terrorism and believed in the
need for a people's party. Already, they were prepared to
countenance the emergence of a State from the revolution. Indeed,
the Russian intellectuals' thirst for efficiency grew unabated
throughout the nineteenth century; while the early generations
had concentrated their attention on problems of distribution,

questions of production and organization came to preoccupy their successors in the 1870s and 80s.[34] The intelligentsia was coming to feel responsible for the future of the Russian economy and for social evolution in general. Its desire to 'revolutionize' was coloured by the desire to do so with some precise end in view.

The emergence of a Russian-style Jacobinism is the more significant in that it coincides with the constitution of an urban proletariat. There were 1,189,000 workers in 1879, and the first wave of strikes occurred in the 1870s (in Saint Petersburg, in the textile industry).[35] The populists agitated among the workers, profiting from this to 'contact' the countryside, with which the latter had remained in close touch. They also managed to convert a number of workers to populism, thus forming a worker élite which, little by little, was to become integrated into the intelligentsia.

But, significantly, the first workers' organizations also began to appear at about this time (the Southern Union of Russian Workers, the Northern Union of Russian Workers, etc.) which, while accepting the intellectuals' ideology (notably Bakuninism), mistrusted the latter and were sometimes even openly hostile. Some of them loudly expressed the wish that the organization of the proletarian masses be left to those primarily concerned.[36] This hostility found concrete expression notably in the refusal to distribute populist pamphlets among the peasants. But, despite this resistance, intellectuals were beginning to organize the workers: Axelrod, Shchedrin and Plekhanov were already active in this field. There were lively disputes between those who remained faithful to populist goals and who were hoping to be able to avoid a capitalist phase in Russia, and those – future social democrats, legal Marxists and left-wing liberals – who thought socialism would result from the evolution of capitalism. The former looked to the countryside, the latter to the towns. However, both were attached to the political forms of revolution and were convinced of the need to *guide* the masses and to institute the socialist State before constructing socialism itself.

This evolution was virtually completed by the early 1880s, and a certain form of populism had been defeated. It was now only a matter of time before the intelligentsia organized itself along the most efficient lines, those closest-linked to the rationale of the rising capitalism. A Marxist group was formed in 1893 in Saint Petersburg which was to direct the workers' circles in the city, and the first congress of the social democrats was held in 1898. So it was Russian Marxism, finally, which provided the intelligentsia with its most appropriate ideological expression.

The gradual replacement of an open, non-authoritarian socialism by an ideology calling for organization and for the seizure of power *on behalf* of the people was no mere accident. It corresponded to the new composition of the revolutionary movement, which itself was the result of the slow transformation of Russian social structures. While in the 1830s and 40s the intelligentsia was identified with a section of the aristocracy (and thus can in no way be said to have been a class), in the following decades it increasingly drew its recruits from the ranks of the *raznochintsy* (*déclassé* intellectuals). These originated in the clergy, the impoverished low-ranking nobility, the *mieshchanstvo* (a statutory category of townspeople : artisans, small shopkeepers); they had broken with their class of origin, and therefore had no status in the eyes of the law. These *déclassé* intellectuals were doubly alienated from the system : they were not officially recognized as a social category and hence they did not constitute an organic part of Russian society. Furthermore, they were acutely aware that their talents and energies were under-employed. They considered themselves utterly superior to all other classes (which is a feature of nihilism) but could find no way of asserting their superiority. The resentment they felt was so powerful that it constituted one of the driving forces of the entire revolutionary movement, but it also made them candidates for leadership of a system which was evolving towards industrial capitalism, in whose framework their professional and intellectual capacities could be profitably employed.

This, then, was the very opposite of the *disinterested*, generous socialism propounded by the pioneers of Russian radical thought: generally unconsciously, their socialism was gradually transformed into a doctrine founded on their eventual accession to power. This process was only completed around the end of the century, with the industrialization of Russia and the constitution of a true intellectual middle class, accelerated by the reforms of the 1860s: abolition of serfdom, creation of a provincial administration, reform of the judicial system. By 1897 the category of *professional intelligentsia* constituted a genuine social class representing some 500,000 persons. Of course, only the lower levels of this class opted for revolution, the 'high intelligentsia' remaining desperately conservative or else turning, at the beginning of the twentieth century, towards liberalism.[37]

The composition of the revolutionary movement evolved as follows: consisting almost entirely of aristocrats in 1830–40, it still contained a good many nobles (though from the lower ranks, the provincial, the impoverished and the modest gentry) in 1860–70, and it was almost entirely made up of commoners drawn from the lower strata of the intelligentsia in 1890–1900.[38]

The radical project's lapse into power ideology, resulting from the evolution of Russia's social structures in the nineteenth century, did not occur without resistance. But the radical alternative was now obliged to take refuge in the writings of sects or in the prophecies of isolated militants: but it continued to exist for all that, and its voice was only stifled with the conclusion of the civil war in the Soviet Union.

Marxism and power: an early critique

Before undergoing a long eclipse, Russian socialism, both populist and anarchist, had developed an early critique of statist systems of thought, and especially Marxism. As we have seen, Herzen was already speaking of Babouvism with respect to the slogans of the new generation of revolutionaries in the 1860s. And in truth Russian socialism in the 1860s and 70s was still divided between two traditions which did not yet appear to be contradictory, but which were subsequently to lead to utterly incompatible theories of revolution.

One of these traditions has its roots in German idealism, in Hegel's phenomenology and utopian French socialism, leading to a socialism that was aristocratic in essence and which later gave birth to populism or, more precisely, to one of its components.

The other tradition arises directly out of eighteenth-century French rationalism and the Great Revolution. While Fourier, and Herzen in his wake, profoundly mistrusted this Revolution, which had done no more than proclaim formal freedoms, the Jacobin and authoritarian socialists, on the other hand, took it as the guiding star in their theoretical heaven. It was the most consistent actors of the 1789 Revolution, those who wished to pursue the process through to its logical conclusion – the Robespierres and the Babeufs – who most profoundly marked the theoreticians of State socialism: Louis Blanc, Weitling, Barbès, Blanqui and, above all, Marx and Engels.

Jacobin socialism established itself very early and very rapidly in Russia (from 1860–5). Tkachev popularized it and adapted it to Russian taste, that is, by amalgamating it with the native populism. All subsequent populism was to share in this ambiguity (for example, 'Narodnaia Volia' which nevertheless, in 1885, called for a revolutionary party *external* to the mass of workers and peasants), which was only cleared up with the organization of a Marxist movement in the 1890s.

But while Marxism only entered Russia as an organized movement in the last decade of the nineteenth century, it was known to certain thinkers. well before this. Tkachev, for example, made historical materialism his own, while Nechaev, after his break with Bakunin, turned to authoritarian communism, drawing inspiration from the *Communist Manifesto*.[39] Above all, a great many Russian exiles abroad, beginning with those famous students in Switzerland, had become thoroughly familiar with a system of thought which inspired one of the factions of the First International. At the same time, these students were involved in all the discussions with the populists then going on, as well as publishing journals and founding revolutionary groups.

In other words, the critique of Marxism was known in Russia well before any party was founded. Bakuninism had begun to spread in Russia from the 1870s onwards, whether directly or through his disciples. Bakunin was not the first to criticize Marx, but his criticisms were the most vigorous, and they are of interest to us more particularly because they form the basis of a *type of thought* perpetuated through anarchism, and because they are remarkably close to those which radicality expresses today. That is to say that one hundred years later, Bakunin's critique seems to us to possess a remarkably prophetic quality.

The Bakuninist critique centres around two main problems: the latent tendencies among the category of intellectuals, and the scientific pretensions of a social theory. The collusion of these two factors seemed to him to constitute the essence of State socialism. Certainly, Bakunin's thesis is not free of all confusion, and he does not distinguish clearly between the negation of the State in general and that of the Marxist State. Most important, he does not illustrate his arguments by means of an analysis of the economic structures of industrial capitalism and of their links with the evolution of social structures. His demonstration is a little abstract from this standpoint, and is reduced to a series of statements of a philosophical order. Nevertheless, these statements *anticipate* the future and, moreover, they were to have a profound influence on subsequent anarchism, and especially on Russian anarchism.

As for intellectuals, or 'savants' as Bakunin called them, they are imbued with a sense of their superiority as a result of their education. From this supposed superiority they conclude that their own future dominance as a class is not only necessary but inevitable. It is this class which 'in the name of its officially recognized erudition and its self-proclaimed intellectual superiority, believes itself destined to rule over the masses'.[40] It is this class which is going to appropriate the State for itself as projected in Marxist theory and thus dominate the masses. The class, then, represents a new aristocracy; and of all aristocracies, this is the most hateful and the most arrogant – it is the last refuge of the spirit of domination.[41]

The Marxist State will signal the reign of the scientific intelligentsia. It will be based on a new hierarchy of real and fictitious savants, and society will be divided into a minority which dominates *in the name of science*, and the immense, uneducated majority. In this case, Bakunin warns, 'Beware of the ignorant masses'.[42]

For, and this is the second aspect of this critique, we are not dealing with just any tyranny: the one in question is going to claim that its justification lies in science. But science as such cannot predict the future, no more than it can legitimize a social regime. For Bakunin it is the action of men, their constant desire for liberation, and not intellectual schemas, which makes history. But intellectuals have seized upon scientific certitudes as though they were a new religion: their positivism is merely at the service of their political ambitions. The 'doctrinaire revolutionaries' see the revolution as opening up vast career prospects for their talents.[43] Believing they understand the true interests of the people better than the people themselves, they assume that their scientific knowledge places them above the people.[44]

Despite its prophetic foresight, Bakunin's analysis was never more than rudimentary; he clearly saw that the intelligentsia is the 'quintessence and the scientific expression of the bourgeois spirit and bourgeois interests' but does not pursue his reasoning any further than that. Notably, he failed to establish the class character of the intelligentsia (he spoke alternatively of caste, class, etc.) and, more especially, he failed to determine its function in the process of capitalist production. But he had initiated an analysis which was to be taken up by his disciples: in Russia it served to clarify the role and ambitions of social democracy. From this point of view, Bakunin was undeniably a precursor and he transmitted to the Russian anarchists at the beginning of the twentieth century a specific analysis of Marxism, an analysis dealing with the predominance of intellectuals in the revolutionary movement and their political ambitions, along with a deep mistrust of scientific theories of social evolution.[45]

It must be said in Bakunin's defence that he did not have occasion to observe the rise of powerful political parties under the influence of Marxism. True, he had a foretaste of centralizing tendencies in the intrigues and manoeuvrings within the General Council of the International Working Men's Association (though he himself was not entirely innocent of all predilection for organization and authoritarianism!). Furthermore, German socialism, even its ideologically watered-down form, was to bear out more than one of his forecasts. Russian social democracy eventually took a rather different turn: all the centralizing and authoritarian potential of Marxism was realized to the utmost. It was against this that Bakuninist-inspired criticism hit out with all its might. From the point of view that concerns us here, namely the permanence of certain themes, this critique found a ferocious advocate in Machajski.

The man who so successfully polished up and publicized Bakunin's intuition was paradoxically neither a Bakuninist, nor even an anarchist. Jan Waclaw Machajski was born at Pinczow (in the Russian part of Poland) in 1867, and he died in total obscurity in Moscow in 1926. His petit-bourgeois origins, a petit bourgeoisie constantly threatened with proletarianization and prepared to stop at nothing to avoid it, provided him with an insider's knowledge of the poor intelligentsia. At the cost of immense effort and privation he managed to complete his secondary education and to get into a university. His fate might have been very different: he might easily have been obliged to seek work as a manual labourer in order to feed his mother and his brothers. So he had known both misery and the pride of those who escape it.

At university, Machajski became an intellectual and threw himself into politics. Following a nationalist phase, he proclaimed himself a social democrat. His Marxist education would appear to have been solid, and he showed a marked preference for political economy, even if his writings in this field are not exactly dazzlingly clear. Naturally enough prison and deportation to Siberia (1892–1903) earned him his wings as a fully fledged revolutionary – as was almost inevitable given the vigilance of the tsarist police. After which he lived underground before emigrating in 1911, finally returning to Russia in April 1917. Machajski wrote his principal work in Siberia, and the rest of his life was devoted to expanding and correcting this work.[46]

The central theme recurring throughout his writings is that socialism is the ideology of a new class seeking power, the *intelligentsia*. Socialism presents itself in the form of a doctrine of liberation and expropriation. And it certainly did seek to expropriate the capitalists, but with the intention of taking their place in the seat of power.

The class of 'mental workers' includes all those who live by their technical or scientific knowledge. It is a category opposed to manual workers. White-collar workers, members of the professions as well as professional revolutionaries, all belong to this category. The intelligentsia emerged as a class alongside the development of industrial society: it is linked to the process of industrialization in modern capitalist economies. But intellectuals are distinguished from entrepreneurs, bankers and shopkeepers (who, naturally, do not work with their hands) in that they have no capital available to them in the form of stockholdings, machinery or cash. They do, on the other hand, possess another perhaps just as valuable form of capital: their *intellectual capital*. This is their education, their years of study, paid for by the labour of the workers.[47]

In Machajski's view, the intelligentsia did not seek to destroy capitalism, but merely to take the place of the bourgeoisie. The latter was now so decadent that it was no longer able to feed its own slaves, nor even to defend its position as the dominant class. The new class of technicians, administrators and savants would institute a rational economy free from economic crises and unemployment. This class was familiar with the mysteries of modern economics and industrial management. It followed from this that the entire history of the nineteenth-century socialist movement was seen as that of a class in quest of power. Furthermore, Machajski was convinced that the capitalist bourgeoisie was diminishing in numbers, and thus flatly contradicted Marx's thesis concerning the increasing proletarianization of the middle and petit bourgeoisie. He believed, on the contrary, that the latter was constantly increasing in number, developing hand in hand with the rise of the industrial economy.

In order to achieve its ambition – the seizure of power – the new dominant class needed allies. As the enemy of the capitalist class, and seeking to grab hold of its State, it may have given the impression that it stood on the side of the proletariat. It may have appeared to be a revolutionary force, but this was only an appearance; it needed the workers in its struggle against its enemies. But in dispossessing the entrepreneur, the intelligentsia had no intention of throwing the engineer, the technician or the accountant out of the factory along with the boss. On the contrary, they were to remain at their posts and to maintain their wage differentials, while the workers would go on being exploited as before. This difference in income was not determined by any qualitative difference in the work accomplished, but by the class situation of the mental workers.

By fighting side-by-side with the intelligentsia for a political revolution the workers were quite simply preparing the ground for a new set of masters for themselves. Under cover of the struggle for national liberation (as in Poland), the parliamentary game or the demand for political freedoms, the intelligentsia was seeking to strengthen and extend the range of its privileges as well as to improve its economic situation. The struggle for political democracy provided the manual worker with nothing in return.

Marx, on the contrary, stated that the proletariat should constitute itself as a political class, electing representatives and entering the State institutions, for time was on its side. Economic evolution would exacerbate the objective contradictions of the capitalist system, leaving the road to the dictatorship of the proletariat wide open. But Machajski claimed that these Marxian predictions had turned out false. It was not true to say that the emancipation of the proletariat *automatically* lay at the end of the historical process. What was true, on the other hand, was that the new class could only attain power when the economic conditions were ripe: which accounts for Marx's emphasis on the 'maturing process' of economic conditions. The enunciation of 'laws' of social evolution was not the social science of modern society, but its ideology. Its so-called scientific character served merely to mystify the workers by preaching patience to them and advising them to engage in long-term political struggle alongside the intellectuals. Once the latter had seized power, they would use Marxism as a drug to induce the workers to accept their new masters. In other words, Marxism was seen here as a religion: the heavenly empire was replaced by the end of exploitation – in some distant future; meanwhile, its role is to justify present oppression.[48]

The unbridled exploitation practised under the socialist regime would be explained and justified by 'objective laws', by the material necessities of the transition to full communism. The worker may be cast in the role of humanity's liberator, but in the meantime he is obliged to submit to the laws of historical necessity, which, in the final analysis, turn out to be no more than the laws of spoliation.

Machajski takes as his canvas the social history of the nineteenth century. He sees here the rise of a class possessing the attributes of all power-seeking classes: ideology, leadership, strategy. Does this mean that the emergence of the intellectual class obliterates the class struggle or nullifies the revolutionary praxis of the proletariat? Not at all. At certain points in time these classes have even united in a common struggle against capitalism. But the events of 1848 mark a decisive split between manual workers and intellectuals. The latter changed sides and turned against the workers, thereby showing their true colours, and their real interests. The intellectuals had glimpsed the spectre of revolution in 1848 and were frightened, for they had everything to lose. Thenceforth, socialism ceased to preach revolution, calling instead for reforms and political democracy. It shrank from forcing open a door it might never be able to close. From revolution and the classless society, its objectives were scaled down to political democracy, the collective ownership of industry and a hierarchical system. In other words, even if in the long term it continued to hope for economic and social transformations, it limited its short-term aims to the seizure of power. Which is why it has always tried to channel workers' revolts towards political demands that are of no benefit whatsoever to the workers themselves.

Thus, says Machajski, an attempt was made to divert the great workers' strike in Lodz in 1902.[49] The strikers were masters of the town for several days while the socialists proclaimed patriotic slogans, as if the workers had a fatherland of their own or were interested in the adoption of a political constitution. On the contrary, it was the intelligentsia which would have benefited directly from all these transformations: the national framework and public liberties suited it down to the ground, not to mention the fact that economies can be run more efficiently under a democratic regime.

The workers are drawn into a struggle which has nothing to do with them. Some of them – the better-paid, hoping to rise in society – join the ranks of the social democrats, having already become members of the intelligentsia and wishing to defend their own interests. The rest, the mass, would only benefit from a social and economic revolution, which can only be achieved by direct action at the base – by means of economic strikes. This is precisely what happened in 1905, when these strikes broke out in direct contradiction to the wishes of the bourgeoisie and those of the socialists, who were calling for political revolution. But the workers have nothing to gain from swapping autocracy for an elected government.[50] Theirs is an *economic* struggle against the bourgeoisie.

On examination, the constructive aspects of Machajski's thought emerge as rather naive. He placed all his confidence in strictly economic demands; the only thing that counted in his view was the improvement of the worker's material conditions. He believed that, with growing income, the worker would inevitably pay for a more complete education for his children who, thus supplied with an 'intellectual capital', would themselves become white-collar workers. Having presented Marxism as a caricature of nineteenth-century scientific positivism, Machajski himself fell victim to the belief in the power of education and schooling to cure all the ills of society.

He does not deny the importance of the revolutionary organization in achievement of these goals, far from it. He dreamed of a universal *workers' conspiracy*,[51] which would stir up increasingly bitter strikes, ultimately culminating in a general strike. This would place the workers in a position to exert pressure on governments and employers to obtain equality of income with the intellectuals.[52]

We can see the extent to which Machajski adopted and developed Bakunin's critique of Marxism and the revolutionary intelligentsia – without ever actually quoting his predecessor. He must at least have read Bakunin, if only during his time at Warsaw University, for Bakunin's writings were widely read by students in the 1880s. People have even tried to present Machajski as an anarchist or a revolutionary syndicalist; in fact, though, he was an isolated figure on the political scene of his time. Although he shared many of the ideas of contemporary revolutionary syndicalism, he totally disagreed with it over the central notion of the union, instead of the party, as the organ of the workers' interests.[53] Similarly, and despite the fact that his thinking had several points in common with anarchism, he did not believe that the anarchists were prepared to work for the economic demands of the proletariat: they too were fighting for 'liberty', and thought of a general strike as nothing more than a peaceful demonstration. Finally, Machajski rejected the position of the libertarians concerning the State for, in his opinion, it was useless to attack political power directly, since it was only a reflection of the economic structures of society. He thought, furthermore, that even an anarchist revolution would place the intelligentsia in power.[54]

He was an isolated figure with few disciples, and those who did follow him for a while ended up by leaving him for anarchism and, after the October Revolution, sided with the Bolsheviks. At least Machajski, on his return to Russia, had the bitter satisfaction of seeing his predictions come true, remarking that even after the disappearance of the capitalist bourgeoisie the workers did not have a government of their own, despite the fact that they were now free to elect their representatives. Power had devolved upon the intellectuals, and these were concerned with defending their own interests.[55]

But even his unfaithful disciples propagated his ideas, and these, it seems, enjoyed a certain vogue for a while. Novomirski, for example, took up Machajski's critique of the revolutionary intelligentsia, holding that the monopoly of knowledge was the greatest enemy of human freedom, and that the intellectual class possessing this monopoly had emerged at the same time as the State and property.[56] Curiously, Machajski even found a number of adepts within the ranks of the Bolshevik party, and the left opposition included at least two groups, after 1917, defending positions close to his own : the 'Workers' Truth' and the 'Workers' Group'.

Machajski was influenced by Bakunin, as were, even more noticeably, the Russian anarchists, although he was not, properly speaking, an anarchist himself. Anarchism developed in the tsarist empire as a response to the generalization of an essentially urban industrial economy. The first groups consisted of workers and students, both these categories being directly affected by the recurrent cycles of crises and unemployment. Solidly organized groups were to be found as early as 1903, but it was in 1905–7 that these circles, originating in the western and south-western provinces of the empire, began to spread throughout all industrial centres and towns of any importance. A relative decline followed this brief flowering, due to a wave of repression in the wake of strikes and uprisings. Many anarchists chose to emigrate, and they continued their activities, centred around the publication of journals and propaganda pamphlets (New York, Paris and Geneva were the principal centres of exiled Russian anarchism). Russian libertarians returned *en masse* with the February and October Revolutions, throwing themselves body and soul into the immense revolutionary tidal wave sweeping over the country.

One cannot really claim that Russian anarchism is the direct heir to a single tradition such as populism or Bakuninism, for example. Its origins are complex and manifold but, and this is worth noting, the movement arose spontaneously in working-class circles in response to a capitalism that was advancing by giant strides, trailing with it its cohort of misery, injustice and exploitation. Unlike the Marxists or the populists, then, the anarchists were not a group of intellectuals looking for recruits for the revolution but small circles of workers resolved to take action. Thus, the libertarian movement was practical before it became theoretical. Entirely concerned with problems of action (strikes, raids, terrorism), it clashed violently with social democracy, accusing the latter of temporizing and of intellectualism.[57]

There was no question, at this stage at least, of discussing the class nature of Russian Marxists; certainly anarchist revolutionaries suspected the latter of harbouring political ambitions, but they made no advance on Bakunin's analyses. Their criticisms were aimed more at tactical questions: parliamentarianism (participation in the Duma), non-violent means of struggle (propaganda, organization) in preference to revolutionary violence.[58]

Paradoxically, the spokesmen for the radical analysis of the Marxist movement were to be found within the social-democratic movement itself. This developed slowly at leadership level from the 1880s onwards. The forerunners, Axelrod, Plekhanov and Zasulich, were former populists who had broken with a certain revolutionary past. Simultaneously, they discovered the writings of Marx and Engels and the workers' movement which was beginning to organize in the course of the 1870s. These early theoreticians of Russian social democracy were also propagandists and leaders: they were to be seen on the occasion of strikes, playing the role of adviser (not always heeded) and 'guide' to the workers in the big cities. Having lost their faith in the revolutionary potential of the peasant masses, they convinced themselves, with the aid of Marxism, that the industrial proletariat was the historic instrument of the revolution.

Marxism in the Russia of the 1890s was divided into two fundamental tendencies: that which, on the one hand, drew a clear distinction between the economic struggle of the proletariat and the political struggle of the revolutionary intelligentsia and, on the other hand, the tendency which sought an interpenetration of the two tasks. The economists (as their opponents called them) considered themselves no less Marxist than the social democrats, and their analyses coincided in a number of points. To begin with, they both shared a conception of history in which industrial capitalism figures as an irresistible trend which, sooner or later, would sweep aside all traces of feudalism. Both also agreed in assigning the proletariat the central role in the capitalist phase: as producers they are the true architects of industrialization, but as employees they are fated to be the victims of bourgeois exploitation. And certainly both Lenin (the sworn enemy of economism – see the biting sarcasm of his *What is to be Done?*) and Martinov had no doubt that the inevitable development of capitalism necessitated a certain number of social evils, the fruits of an 'objective' and ineluctable process.[59]

The economists, however, believed that the class struggle *par excellence* lay in the spontaneous economic struggles of the proletariat. For them, the political activities of the radical intelligentsia should merge with the political activities of the liberal opposition: the social revolution could not result from a political struggle against the autocracy. The social democrats, with Lenin foremost, favoured on the contrary giving priority to the political struggle insofar as economic demands irremediably degenerated into trade unionism, i.e. a form of syndicalism perfectly compatible with the bourgeois order.

From 1900 onwards, the hardline social democrats led a ruthless struggle in the columns of *Iskra* against the economists, whose theories were identified with Bernsteinian opportunism. Alongside this, the editorial board of the first *Iskra* (Lenin, Plekhanov, Axelrod, Zasulich, Potressov, Martov) developed a conception of the party that was diametrically opposite to that of the economists: a hierarchized party composed of professional revolutionaries working underground, with a centralized organization, and whose aim would be to *lead* the workers' struggles. That is, in Lenin's conception the proletariat should not only be confined to trade union-type demands, but it should throw its entire weight behind the political struggle against tsarist rule. This view is expressed with greatest vigour in the articles Lenin wrote for *Iskra* (1900–3), in his pamphlet *What is to be Done?* (1902), and in his speeches to the Social Democrats' Congress in 1903.

It was at this point in the discussion that a number of voices were raised within the social-democratic movement and even among the small group of émigrés centred around *Iskra*. These voices were perfectly qualified to criticize Lenin's faction since they belonged to activists with first-hand experience of the way in which these conceptions were incarnated in the everyday practice of social-democratic organization. This critique was rather more pertinent, and less abstract than that put forward by the *Rabochaia Mysl* economists.[60]

What is interesting from the point of view of radical theory is that this critique poses the crucial problem of the nature of Russian socialism – a struggle for power for a single class or a struggle for the liberation of the proletariat – and in so doing places itself at the extreme limits of Marxism. It nevertheless remains within the bounds of the social-democratic movement, refusing from the outset to step beyond the limits. Neither Axelrod nor Trotsky nor Rosa Luxemburg had any quarrel with the conception of the party or with that of the vanguard essential to the class struggle. This is why – as we shall see for Rosa Luxemburg – this dual position (critical and conformist) was to lead to a number of ambiguities and even contradictions. And this was not the last time a lucid and pitiless analysis of the party would lead a Trotsky to contradict himself; a quarter of a century later he himself was to fall into the same trap.

The Congress of the Russian Social Democratic Workers' Party held in 1903 (formally the second) gave rise to a reexamination of the aims and characteristics of Russian socialism. Antagonisms were exacerbated by the factional in-fighting which dominated the entire congress, in the course of which Lenin managed to maintain control of the party's organs by a margin of a few votes. This brazen struggle for power within the party, *before* it even existed formally, aroused the indignation of a number of delegates not yet reconciled to the cold Machiavellianism of the committee men. Later, when the Bolsheviks and Mensheviks had constituted two entirely distinct factions – if not to say parties – theoretical compliments began to be exchanged through the medium of codified invective ('opportunism', 'factionalism', 'rightism', 'revolutionarism', 'Blanquism', etc.) rather than with the support of any fundamental analysis. At this point there was no further disagreement concerning objectives, namely the seizure of power on behalf of the party. The divergences concerned historical tactics, the Mensheviks placing their trust in the spontaneous organizations of the proletariat, infiltrating them if necessary, while the Bolsheviks recognized no organizations other than those subordinated to their own apparatus. The former were somewhat sceptical about their chances of ever coming to power (which earned them a reputation for 'half-heartedness' among the workers); the latter, on the contrary, pushed their voluntarism to the point of adopting the programme of their sworn enemies (the revolutionary socialists), provided the masses accorded them their much-needed support in the march towards the conquest of the State.

However, in 1903–4 the camps were not yet clearly and definitively delimited, and the reaction to the Leninist conception of the party arose spontaneously. True, German social democracy, at the time the most powerful, was hardly a model of 'democratism', but at least it 'had' the masses, and its centralism was concealed behind the existence of hundreds and even thousands of officials which gave the party the illusion of a constant exchange between the base and the summit. Lenin's theses (and already his practice!), by contrast, shocked people with their dogmatism: here was a party made up of a few thousand intellectuals and a handful of workers, most of whom were no longer involved in the productive process, pretending not merely to the leadership of the masses but also to the monopoly of theoretical reflection. It was a strictly hierarchized and centralized party, demanding rigid discipline from its members, and presenting itself as the proletariat's guide, presuming in advance to approve or condemn this same proletariat's struggles. It would have raised a laugh if a certain number of people had not perceived tendencies in it which, on the contrary, called for the utmost gravity.

Their critique was the more clearcut in that they saw before them the concentrate, the essence of social democracy or, more precisely, a social democracy which only existed in essence. In attacking it, these heretics were really hitting out at all forms of State socialism, even if this was not clear to them, whether later or at the time.

In conditions prevailing in tsarist Russia, what could be the meaning of a political struggle? asked Axelrod. Above all this struggle was democratic–bourgeois in character, that is to say it aimed at replacing the feudal monarchy with the reign of the capitalist bourgeoisie. The Russian Social Democratic Workers' Party was engaged in precisely this struggle, and Lenin's conceptions merely accentuated the 'left-wing bourgeois' character of the Party.[61] For, far from drawing inspiration from the masses and going to them to learn about proletarian reality at first hand, Lenin's followers set themselves up as their leaders. But in its social composition, however, the RSWDP was undeniably a bourgeois party, and if the workers supported it and followed its line it was because of the lack of a Western-style liberal bourgeois party on the Russian political scene. For the time being, then, the party was an organization run by the revolutionary intelligentsia, and Lenin's ultra-centralism was likely to perpetuate this state of affairs. There was a great danger, Axelrod pointed out, that the existing party organization and its policies would lead to the emergence of a bourgeois revolution and that alone. He then wondered whether the ideological wrapping (the Party's revolutionary programme) did not conceal an objective content whose fundamental principles remained within the framework of radical democracy.

Axelrod further suspected that what he termed Lenin's organizational utopia (centralism, bureaucracy, the conspiratorial nature of the organization) incarnated a bourgeois ideology. Leading the masses directly, under the tutelage of the Party, into the struggle against the autocracy, he wrote, could only result in the seizure of power by the radical bourgeoisie. He inevitably drew a parallel with the French Revolution of 1789, when the Jacobins, drawing support from the clubs and the *sociétés populaires*, faithfully carried out the policies of the bourgeoisie.[62] In short, behind the élite of professional revolutionaries drawn from the intelligentsia, Axelrod dimly perceived a 'general staff' ready to use the proletarian masses in order to carry out its own revolution, a revolution that would hoist it to power. But the mystique of the Party, of a social-democratic movement whose role is to educate the proletariat, was too powerful for him to be able to follow his line of reasoning through to its logical conclusion. He himself scarcely believed his own warning when he wrote that history might very well play the same trick on the Russian socialists as it played on the French revolutionary bourgeoisie, by dressing up the bourgeois content of the movement in the ideological clothes of radical democracy.

When Trotsky examined the consequences of the decisive congress held in August 1903 he was no less apprehensive. He declared flatly that the workers' movement must eventually transform itself into a 'process of proletarian self-determination'.[63] If this did not happen, he added, Russian social democracy would be seen to have been a historical mistake. But, what was actually going on in AD 1904? The party of the revolutionary intelligentsia was in the process of substituting itself for the proletariat, elaborating its own private theory of revolution, and was attempting to bend the reality of class struggle to this theory. But, Trotsky wrote, history simply does not permit this kind of substitution; the proletarian theory of political development cannot replace a politically developed proletariat. Revolutionary consciousness cannot come to the masses from the outside. It can only come from the objective conditions of their existence. Lenin's party resembled the classical capitalist factory, where a minority gives the orders and the great majority is merely invited to jump to it.

Trotsky went on to situate Lenin in the Jacobin tradition which, he said, represents 'the maximum degree of radicalism a bourgeois society is capable of producing'.[64] It was this underlying Jacobinism which led the Bolshevik leader to believe that the preparation of the proletariat for dictatorship was purely a question of organization; in point of fact, though, his organizational ideas lead to a dictatorship *over* the proletariat. For Jacobinism, like Blanquism, is a bourgeois ideology aiming at nothing more nor less than the construction of a power apparatus.

Already in 1903, Trotsky published a pamphlet comparing Lenin with Robespierre and laying bare Lenin's struggle for power within the party.[65] He went further still in 'Our Political Tasks' and accused Lenin's friends of using Marxism as an ideological veil to hide their bourgeois-revolutionary (Jacobin) role, with which these said friends had become perfectly reconciled. The democratic intelligentsia had adopted Marxism because it provided them with a theoretical base for their struggle for political emancipation.[66] This gave rise to the illusion that it was the social democrats' task to liberate the Russian people, as a certain (Leninist) committee in Odessa proclaimed. Which led Trotsky to comment:

the Odessa Committee has evidently rejected the little notion that the liberation of the people can only come from the people itself as a vestige of *'suivisme'*. Long live the Odessa Committee, the people's 'liberator', which has already liberated the workers of Odessa from the task of having to liberate themselves! Only, one wonders in what way the Odessa Committee's slogan [Long live social democracy, the Russian people's liberator] is better than the promises of the old 'people's heroes', and what reason we have to believe that the 'fighting organization' will really obtain freedom for the people.[67]

In Rosa Luxemburg's case, however, this was no longer a question of tactical criticism, soon to be corrected or retracted. One cannot deny her a certain logic, and a great deal of perseverance, in the defence of her theses. Throughout her career as a social-democrat activist she maintained her hostility towards a certain conception – which today we might term bureaucratic – of the party and of revolutionary organization in general. But if Rosa Luxemburg's qualities lay in her obstinacy, and in her fidelity towards a theory of spontaneity that was ultimately to become identified with her, her critique never attained the radicality of a Trotsky. This was because Rosa Luxemburg's entire life was devoted to the social-democratic movement; outside of this universe neither her activities nor her militant thought were conceivable. Trotsky, on the other hand, was extremely independent-minded. It was no mere accident that he avoided all factions until 1917, and even then he only joined the one he thought most effective. This independence gave him the freedom to vent his violent reactions on every and any concept, however orthodox. But there was another side of the coin; once his anger was past, once his prophetic thunderbolts had been hurled, he was capable – when enjoying ministerial power – of keeping silent when he should have spoken up. Rosa Luxemburg, with her limitations and her quest for orthodoxy and a spiritual family, could be tempted by nothing outside what she believed to be the truth.

Rosa Luxemburg's principal theoretical concern, from *The Mass Strike, the Political Party and the Trade Union* to her final 'Speech' on the programme of the young German Communist Party then in formation, was to reconcile organization, the necessity of a vanguard with the autonomous proletarian dynamic. Perhaps the reason why some people have been attracted to 'Luxemburgism' is that it attempted to reconcile two irreconcilables, resulting in a 'lame synthesis'.[68] In truth, it is not easy to show that the impulses of the masses and their revolutionary practice are both spontaneous and dependent upon a social democracy 'which alone is capable of unleashing this energy and shapes it as a decisive factor in political life'.[69] Nevertheless, the fundamental role which Rosa Luxemburg assigned to their autonomous activity led her to condemn severely parties such as the RSDWP which ignored this aspect. And if she failed to perceive Marxism's role as a mystifying ideology with regard to the ambitions of the intelligentsia, she did believe that the latter's organizational conceptions were incompatible with the ultimate aims of socialism. For her, the existence of an all-powerful central committee ruling over the masses could only amount to the projection, in practice, of pure and unalloyed Blanquism. This seemed to her to stem from Lenin's own definition of the social democrat: 'a Jacobin indissolubly linked to the *organization* of the proletariat henceforth ·*conscious* of its class interests'.[70]

Thus, the kind of discipline practised by Lenin was typically that of the bourgeois State: the central committee controlled the workers, whereas the reverse would have been the case in the Marxist conception of the revolutionary struggle.[71] Too much centralization was liable to place excessive power in the hands of the intellectual leaders of the social-democrat movement, enabling them to further their ambitions. Rosa Luxemburg thought that only the autonomous action of revolutionaries could foil the designs of an ambitious intelligentsia, only too likely, on the morrow of the revolution, to acquire rapidly a bourgeois class content. In other words the dictatorship, as Lenin first conceived and later practised it, was more akin to the Jacobin dictatorship advocated by the Blanquists than to that of the proletariat in its struggle against the bourgeoisie. In these conditions, asked Rosa Luxemburg, will the masses not simply have served as a rung on the ladder to power for a handful of intellectuals? For a dictatorship on the lines of Jacobin hegemony?[72]

The criticisms advanced by Rosa Luxemburg, who was thoroughly familiar with the European social-democratic movement, beginning with the RSDWP,[73] raise a fundamental question concerning the social character of (future) Bolshevik power. In 1918 she urged that the proletariat's duty was to set up a *class dictatorship*, which she opposed to that of a party or of a tiny minority governing in the name of the class. But, like Trotsky later, she reasoned in terms of mistakes, errors, of abuses and even ambitions of certain misguided intellectuals. Her analysis stopped there. Like most Marxists of her generation, she could hardly conceive of socialist revolution without the party's education, inspiration and leadership. She would have liked to change the relationships within the party, to establish a (mythical) fluidity between the leaders and the masses. It seemed to her quite evident that any spontaneous uprising by the proletariat could only be *elementary* and that it would have to ally itself with a group of theoreticians, tacticians and propagandists capable of channeling this revolutionary activity towards social revolution.

In these conditions it is difficult to see how she could have touched on the question of the social character of the 'leaders': if these had their own revolutionary objectives corresponding to their class existence, then their interests would never coincide with those of the proletariat and they would never be in a position to lead the latter towards its goal. And yet, the 'alliance' between intellectuals and workers seemed indispensable, the fusion of revolutionary consciousness and revolutionary energy being as much a dogma for Luxemburg as for her contemporaries. One can see the vicious circle in which she was trapped in spite of herself. From the moment she refused to recognize that the proletariat has a complete existence *for itself*, and hence is fully autonomous, she could not deepen her analysis to the point of penetrating beyond appearances: an intelligentsia capable of being deceived by bureaucratic leaders but which, in any case, is irreplaceable as the vital catalyst in the transformation of social relations.

Any critique that does not reassess the problem of social democracy in its entirety is trapped, right from the outset, within the same vicious circle. However far this critique was developed, whether by Axelrod, Trotsky or Luxemburg, it never aimed at anything beyond, at best, the substitution of one set of leaders for another or, failing that, the improvement of the existing leadership.

Criticism from *within* developed as far as it possibly could, and with an astonishing degree of lucidity, right from the time of the first congress (1903) and the discussions then taking place concerning the Leninist line. All the vices of bureaucratism, appointments from above, manipulation of congress delegates, were roundly condemned; and the arrogance, intolerance and stifling discipline of Leninism were shown up indignantly. As was to happen later, from 1920 onwards, the only solution that the best and most disinterested among the social democrats could come up with involved no more than a change of 'political line', 'increased democracy' or more real 'contact' with the masses. A clear understanding of the situation as a whole – of the *narrow interdependence* that existed between the interests of the intelligentsia, their social and economic role in a capitalism made up of large units and bureaucratic methods, hierarchy, intolerance and contempt for the masses – was denied even the most perceptive of the social democrats.

We have seen that the pre-populist period of Russian socialism was rich in warnings and prophecies. We have also observed that radicality, while almost entirely cut off from the realities of political struggle, was nonetheless preserved in a number of tiny circles, or even in the writings of isolated individuals.

Populism, in the strict sense of the term – the movement that began with the 'Go to the People' campaigns – introduced a period of activism, but it led to an impoverishment of radical thought. The rise of the intellectual class parallel to the development of industrial capitalism in Russia highlighted the problem of organization. This was resolved the moment Plekhanov, Axelrod and others went to 'help' the workers conduct their strikes. The practical problem was dealt with before the theoretical one: it was only afterwards that people began to codify and conceptualize their habit of placing themselves at the head of the proletariat.

When former populists began spreading Marxism in Russia and later, in exile, teaching Marxism to apprentice revolutionaries, all they were doing by this time was to drape the intelligentsia in those famous ideological vestments mentioned by Marx, whose function was not merely to mystify the proletariat but also to conceal their true situation from them. A struggle for the hearts and minds of the intelligentsia itself then ensued. Torn between liberalism, constitutionalism and the various forms of Marxism (legal, economist, social-democrat) or even reluctant to abandon populism, the different fractions of the intelligentsia made their choices according to their precise position within the middle classes, their temperament and historical optimism or fatalism. This was what the in-fighting that took place within this class in the course of the 1890s was about: all were agreed, however, that the principal objective was the emancipation of the working class. Alongside the 'struggle for the liberation of the working class' group (Leninist) we find the 'workers' self-liberation' group (economist) while 'Workers' Thought' was akin to 'Workers' Newsletters'. The problem was whether the political struggle should be carried on parallel to workers' demands or in alliance with the proletariat; was one to be satisfied with a parliamentary regime (the liberals' position) or should one start preparing the battle for socialism straightaway (the social democrat's position)?

The historical vision of all concerned imperatively assumed the development and the flowering of capitalism with all its consequences (and here they began to shift away from populism, which preferred to skip the urban industrial phase).[74] The first point on which the social democrats began to drift away from the economists, the legal Marxists, etc., concerned the need to draw the proletariat into the political struggle against the tsarist autocracy or, to use their opponents' paraphrase, against the tsarist police. But, if drawing the proletariat into a task that, historically, fell to the bourgeoisie constituted an initial rallying cry around the social-democratic standard, the *manner* in which this 'alliance' was to be concluded inevitably provoked fresh divergences, this time inside the movement.

Following a period of realignment inside the intelligentsia, a battle for partisan loyalty broke out, in which the working class was intimately involved. This stage was inaugurated around 1903, and it witnessed the splitting of the social democrats into Bolsheviks and Mensheviks. But no-one dreamed for a moment of calling upon the workers to umpire the quarrel which, both in name and in the final analysis, concerned their own liberation! The combat was fought out with the intelligentsia's own esoteric weapon – theoretical argument. And this is only right when one considers that what was at stake was the bourgeois revolution and hence, in the first place, the destiny of the intelligentsia as a class.

Machajski showed this very clearly when he predicted that socialism would usher in the reign of the new bourgeoisie – the mental workers. His critique, when set alongside those of Axelrod, Trotsky and Luxemburg, illustrates this remarkable phenomenon, namely that even before the 1905–7 revolution, organized Marxism was being brought face to face with its ultimate objectives. On the one hand, Machajski winkled out the class dimension of the Marxist intelligentsia; on the other hand, the internal critique of the social-democratic movement, having shrewdly perceived the autonomous nature of all proletarian liberation, went utterly astray regarding the historical significance of the social-democratic movement.

It was only after the Bolshevik Revolution that the radical critique once more became free to develop beyond this stage. This was because while, prior to this, all judgments and analyses were founded solely on the dream of power, power was achieved in 1917 and thenceforth became a reality. Predictions that had earlier been couched in terms of underlying tendencies could now at last give way to the examination of an historical incarnation : the Soviet State.

3   Council communism

The theory of workers' councils originated in the new forms of industrial conflict which burgeoned during and immediately after the First World War. Among these new forms we can (already) mention wildcat strikes, factory occupations and the formation of committees of shop-floor delegates.

The whole question of the council phenomenon is shrouded in myths and mistaken interpretations, which induce caution. For example, while we generally tend to associate the soviet with the Russian Revolution, the original concept of the council – based on a radical critique of the classical theory of party and unions – was not formulated in Russia (either in 1905 or in 1917). Again, for a long time the councils were presented as an institution springing forth spontaneously from the revolutionary mass movement, incarnating the autonomy of the masses relative to the proletariat's own organizations. This is only completely true in the case of the 1905–7 Russian Revolution, and one should bear in mind that the unions were still only in their infancy at the time, while the Bolsheviks were unrepresented in the factories. In 1917, on the other hand,[1] the councils were of a very different nature, more closely resembling the type then prevalent in Central Europe. Here, reality was a far cry from legend. For councils of all kinds were formed on the initiative of one or another of the nuances of the socialist movement, or were at least controlled by them. [2]

One cannot, therefore, claim that the councils reflected an entirely autonomous reality or practice. In any case, this would have been inconceivable at a time – to use a Leninist expression – when even social-democratic consciousness was far from affecting all working-class milieux.

But as with all genuinely revolutionary epochs, the period 1914–21 brought with it both topian transformations of reality as well as a projection of more profound demands for emancipation which were to remain within the realm of utopia.[3] In the world of concrete phenomena one has only to think of the immense upheaval which occurred in manners, in the most deeply rooted beliefs, in habits and customs unchanged all through the nineteenth century. One should also bear in mind the development of new practices, such as active State intervention in social and economic life, the growing involvement of women of all classes in the world of work, their political as well as familial self-assertion; the end of the gold standard and of price stability, the assertion of national rights, the collapse of feudal systems (in Eastern and Central Europe). These are just some of the factors signalling a total break with the past.

Social relations had inevitably undergone a profound transformation. A whole generation had been mobilized, whether in the army, in munitions factories, agriculture or hospitals. Uprooted once and for all, it was to prove far less submissive, much more turbulent than its predecessors. Above all, it was thrust into a world of anxiety and economic uncertainty in which it was far more prone to contestation. Nor would the spirit of contestation, of revolt even, spare the workers' organizations themselves, for their attitude and behaviour in the course of this period was gravely to sap the capital of trust they had built up among militants in the pre-war era.

Paradoxically, the unions and workers' parties actually grew in numbers and discipline immediately after the war, at a time when their authority was becoming more readily questioned. The haste with which workers' and socialist leaders had rallied to their national flags, the collaboration between unions and civil and military authorities to break wildcat strikes during the war, provided working-class consciousness with a heavy dose of scepticism. So, through their new forms of action, workers in fact gave vent to a whole range of utopian aspirations made possible by secular subjection. Thus, at one and the same time, authoritarian-type apparatuses and ideologies gained in followers while losing in credibility. The first leaf of this diptych held sway for half a century, with the ascendency of the workers' leadership becoming *topia*; but today we are witnessing the emergence of a quest for autonomy which was already to be found in embryo in the years 1917–21.

The institutions which arose in this period, and which constitute a positive innovation by comparison with what had by now become a veritable working-class custom, partake of this anti-nomic duality. For the most part, the workers' council was under the control of syndicalist or socialist militants. But as a *project* (and the spontaneous and unpredictable conditions of its appearance bear witness to this), the workers' council is a concrete utopia, overriding and denying the circumstances of its institutionaliza-tion. It contains, in the form of (not immediately realizable) vir-tualities, the demand for autonomy currently thrusting itself into the forefront of attention.

The originality of the council movement lay in its perception of the drift of future evolution. Although its theoretical work was founded on indications only, it was certainly not based on illusion. True, it was difficult to avoid triumphalism entirely in the condi-tions of revolutionary ferment of those years. Some even went so far as to identify any workers' council with some form of opposi-tion to the established workers' leaderships, thus stumbling into a dogmatism which has marked the major part of council ideology. Consequently, it is worth taking a look at the real context within which these strikes and councils, mutinies and revolts grew up before going on to deal with the theory of councils and the circum-stances of its birth in detail.

The First World War and the emergence of new forms of workers' struggle

The situation in most of the belligerent countries was pre-revolutionary, if not revolutionary. But setting aside Russia, we find three types of situation. In Germany and Austria, councils covered the entire territory and assumed at least partial power; in Bavaria and Hungary they wielded formal political and social power at the summit; while in England and Italy, even if the councils had no political power, they nonetheless developed into a far from negligible council movement.

Workers' councils made their appearance in Austria in November 1918, at the same time as in Germany. They rapidly spread to cover much of the country; but very nearly all of these organizations were formed on the initiative of the socialist party, and socialist militants were well represented on the councils' highest bodies – the executive committees. Furthermore, and here lies the main difference with Germany, the Austrian councils were never once in a position to seize power. The revolution, if revolution there was, occurred within the framework of State and parliamentarianism.[4]

In Germany, on the other hand, the councils were constitutional in character. The first occasion was on 10 November 1918, when the Greater Berlin Workers' and Soldiers' Council confirmed the composition of the new government, which was followed by the transfer of executive power to the government on 23 November.[5] Similarly, a month later the Pan-German Congress of Councils handed over its powers to a future Constituent Assembly, for which it then voted.

But reality was more complex than these juridical forms suggest. The situation arose out of the balance of political power and of the very nature of the workers' councils in Germany. The latter made their appearance in the wake of the strike movement and the army mutinies which hit the country as from 1917. These strikes were aimed at employers who refused to increase wages despite rising prices; and at the government, which was doing nothing to halt the war, but they were also directed against social democracy and the unions. As far back as August 1914 the SPD (the German Social Democratic Party) had adopted a policy of collaboration with the imperial government; it was not long before the party came to be seen as both a hostage and a guarantee for the government. True, the leaders favoured a 'war to the finish'. As for the unions, they had undertaken to avoid all industrial conflicts for the duration of the war. And it was not an uncommon sight to see the *Generalkommission* (their supreme body) making common cause with employers and the military authorities in order to smash a work stoppage. As a result, the wave of strikes affecting Germany from April 1917 onwards took on a distinctly anti-union colouring; wildcat strikes broke out with growing frequency right up until the armistice, only to spread with even greater vigour from that moment on.[6]

These 'illegal' actions swept the old union structures clean out of the factories. In their place workers proceeded to elect delegates who would be answerable to the rank and file, and who were hostile to the existing hierarchy. The delegates met in works committees (*Betriebsräte*), prefiguring the workers' councils proper, elected on the same basis but for the purposes of political representation.[7] While one can point to the existence of councils as early as spring 1917, it was only in the autumn of 1918 that they began to spread so widely that, in the eyes of public opinion, they came to incarnate the mass revolutionary movement.[8] It was the naval mutinies which sparked off a movement that had been simmering for at least a year; civilians were quick on the uptake and, starting with the major ports (Kiel, Hamburg, Bremen), each town, each region began electing workers' and soldiers' – or workers' and peasants' – councils.

In the beginning there can be no doubt that these councils arose spontaneously, but the situation soon settled down, and by December 1918–January 1919 it was already possible to take stock of things and to distinguish three categories of council, depending upon the size of the locality.

In most small and medium-sized towns the initiative was taken by the local SPD organization (generally in collaboration or in agreement with the local branch of the unions), either by arranging for the election of a council on a show of hands at a mass rally, or by designating the candidates itself. In rural areas councils were often formed without socialist participation, and bourgeois or agrarian delegates were not infrequent.[9]

In the big towns, notably the industrial ones, the SPD allied with the USPD (independent social democratic party, offspring of wartime pacifism) in order to control a council or to form it. Where the parties did not have the initiative, they arranged to have themselves coopted on to executive committees in sufficient numbers, even when the councils were elected by factory delegates – the purest form of workers' democracy. In some large towns, however, it was the 'left-wing radicals', the revolutionary wing of social democracy, who wielded the predominating influence. But, in general, the SPD was in control of the council organizations.[10]

From the point of view of the country as a whole, two councils assumed particular importance: the Greater Berlin Council and the Pan-German Council, constituted on the basis of nationwide elections. Both were led by social-democrat majorities. Thus, of the 489 delegates to the Congress of Workers' and Soldiers' Councils (16–20 December 1918), 292 belonged to the SPD, eighty-four to the USPD, while only ten were Spartakists.

One may conclude, from this rapid survey, that the spread of councils did not in itself express any project going beyond the establishment of a democratic republic within the framework of the capitalist regime.[11] While it is true that, from mid-November on, councils began replacing regional and local authorities all over Germany, the administration nevertheless stayed at its posts and the social power of the landowners and industrialists remained intact. It was within the framework of this power system that the change in political regime took place; a change sanctioned by the councils, moreover, since their national executive handed over the job of drawing up a constitution for the German Republic to a parliamentary assembly.

The fact that the councils were almost entirely dominated by the SPD was due to the existing balance of power between the various parties and revolutionary groups. But if the councils had no reality *outside* the parties and unions whose representatives populated their executive committees, this was due less to the existence of the workers' organizations than to the inevitable limitations upon any attempt to transcend social-democratic consciousness at the time. Radicality was as yet able to express itself only in terms of the *project* of factory committees and workers' councils.

One is inclined to wonder whether this was equally true of those countries where the councils wielded both political and social power, as was the case for a brief period in Bavaria and in Hungary.

The Bavarian monarchy fell on 7 November, and Kurt Eisner proclaimed the republic, which he intended should be organized along democratic lines. Five months later he was replaced by a first republic of soviets presided over by Ernst Toller, who in turn gave way to a second republic of soviets with the communist Eugene Leviné at its head. The role of the councils in this merry-go-round of regimes was reduced to that of sounding board for the avatars of this inter-party struggle. For, here again, real power was in the hands of the SPD and the USPD, soon to be joined by the recently formed communist party. Thus, both Eisner's provisional government and Leviné's council of people's commissars resulted from a coalition of parties which held together thanks to the lynchpin role played by the independent socialists. Despite the presence of anarchists, the councils themselves reflected these partisan cleavages.[12]

The situation was different in Hungary insofar as the socio-economic regime itself was shaken. Nationalization and land redistribution measures were planned, even if they did not lead to genuine socialization during the 133 days of the Hungarian Soviet Republic (22 March–2 August 1919).

The significance of the councils in Hungary should be analysed in the light of the external situation on the one hand, and of the political forces at work on the other. It differs before and after the establishment of the Soviet regime.

The emergence of councils during the war[13] corresponds to the growing radicalization in the belligerent countries. From

November 1917 onwards, violent strikes and sabotage occurred in the principal factories, and a general strike in June 1918 brought the economy to a standstill. These were very bitter strikes, whose political character was more pronounced than in other countries. Continued pressure from the workers led to increasing radicalization. In January 1919 several factories were confiscated from their owners and run by the local workers' councils.[14] Despite the existence of an aggressive minority which directly attacked the unions, the latter had long been solidly established and constituted a vital cog in working-class life. Together with the socialist party they controlled the Workers' Soviet of Budapest, the only one to play an important political role. Thus it backed Count Karolyi's government, in which the socialists were represented. It approved all the measures presented by the social-democrat leaders, notably the alliance with the communist group, which was demanding the establishment of a council regime.

In this respect, the establishment of such a regime in Hungary looks rather like an operation artificially grafted by the propagandists grouped around Béla Kun, who had received some political training during their captivity in Russia. Faced with the threat of invasion by the Entente powers, the socialists formed a government together with the communist leaders, hauling the latter from the gaols into which they had allowed them to be thrown shortly before.

The supreme authority in the new republic was represented by the Budapest Council. Following the April 1919 elections, its executive committee contained fifty-six socialists and twenty-four communists out of eighty members.[15] So the new regime rested, right from the outset, upon a compromise between the communists and socialists, the latter deciding in all disputed cases.[16]

Paradoxically, the reason why the socialists accepted what might otherwise look like a very poor bargain, even though they were both stronger and better established than the communists, was that they were being attacked from the left for their lack of a foreign policy capable of satisfying the nationalism of the majority of citizens. The Bolshevik project of creating a soviet regime as in Russia was shelved; Béla Kun, the Commissar for Foreign Affairs, attempted to extricate Hungary from her tricky position vis-à-vis the Entente powers and the territorial claims of her neighbours. Having failed to untie this Gordian knot, Kun and his group were obliged to step down, having also shown themselves incapable of imposing a 'subjective' solution in a country where the 'objective' situation (the importance of rural areas, solid union implantation and a very moderate socialist party) was unfavourable to them.

On the local scene, the old administration continued to exercise its authority right through this period; nationally speaking, the councils had no existence outside the parties, whose instruments they were.

While in Hungary, despite its 'soviet' regime, there was no council ideology distinct from Béla Kun's Bolshevik schema, England experienced a genuine movement in favour of free and autonomous workers' expression. This movement, known as the 'shop stewards' movement', combined two different phenomena.

On the one hand, before the war, the socialist Labour Party and the Guild Socialists had been spreading propaganda in favour of workers' control. This was still only a timid plan to give workers some say in the running of their factory, and although both projects stipulated that the workers would be represented by their unions, the latter were resolutely opposed to any such scheme (as was the majority socialist party, the Labour Party).[17] But the idea was so well received by the metalworkers and miners that the Trades Union Congress ended by adopting, in 1918, the principle of joint control in those industries whose nationalization it was demanding.

On the other hand, the wartime period was also a time of great agitation, particularly among munitions workers and miners. Most union leaders backed the National Government and its wartime policies right up to the hilt.[18] Since, on top of this, the unions had undertaken to abstain from all strike-backed wage claims, the workers felt obliged to turn to their shop stewards (originally little more than union recruiting agents, having no power to negotiate) in order to make themselves heard.

Discontent came to a head in 1915 following two initiatives by unions that had subscribed to an 'industrial truce' and had turned a blind eye to the practice of 'dilution' (employing semi- or unqualified workers to do qualified work) in munitions factories. The Clydeside metalworkers' strike (early 1915) confirmed the shop stewards in their new and 'illegal' role; now that they were organized into workers' committees they constituted the expression of rank-and-file opposition to all authority, whether employers' or unions'.

The Clydeside strike was followed by disputes in other sectors of the economy. An uninterrupted succession of work stoppages and violent confrontations took place between the outbreak of the great May 1917 strike (which had broken out in the munitions industry) and the miners' strike of 1920; the shop stewards played a leading role in all these disputes.[19] Each factory, each region set up its own workers' committee, delegates being elected on a non-union basis. In most cases, these movements originating in the rank-and-file clashed with the existing organizations.[20]

This phenomenon became very widespread in the first three or four years of its existence. Particularly vigorous among the metal-workers, the movement expanded after 1918. Regional committee leaders began to set up a national structure as early as November 1916, and by August 1917 a conference was attended by twenty-three committees. A national council was elected, but the committees preserved a good deal of autonomy.

As for the themes most frequently discussed by the shop stewards' movement, we should distinguish between those which are consubstantial so to speak, with the movement itself, demanding direct rank-and-file representation, the control of industry by the workers themselves and even the negation of the capitalist State, and those which were soon to be propagated by the national leadership. The latter were more politically marked in character and were to popularize slogans originating from the Russian Bolsheviks. As time went on, the distance separating the initial impetus and the movement's national council widened. While the rank-and-file movement declined following the end of the war, most of the delegates and committees being absorbed into the unions, the leaders, who now constituted a distinct group, agitated in favour of joining the communist party. We have come a long way from the ideological premises of 1916–19 (worker's control, setting up of factory organizations, negation of the State). The slogans had now become: conquest of the State, construction of State socialism, construction of a communist party. This evolution was complete by 1921, when the National Conference of the Shop Stewards' Movement declared that the proletariat alone was incapable of managing production without the socialist State; the unions were rehabilitated, and political action in the narrow sense of the term came to the fore.[21]

As can be seen, the shop stewards' and rank-and-file movement only represented something really radical and innovative in its first years, before it came to incarnate a precise political project. Its limitations arose out of the circumstances which gave birth to it: the complex problem of dilution, which was resolved when the unions returned to their restrictive, corporatist attitudes following the end of hostilities. At all events, the limits to the radical consciousness of the movement were those of a highly stratified working class. It would be another half-century before the re-emergence of wildcat strikes and rebellious shop stewards expressing the demands for autonomy of a levelled and homogeneous class.

In Italy, the rising revolutionary wave gave births to some original thinking on the role of councils in the workers' struggle. The post-war period especially was marked by disputes between workers and bosses. Strikes intensified towards the middle of 1919 (metalworkers in the north, agricultural labourers, typesetters, textile workers, sailors).[22] The economic crisis, unemployment, the problems of demobilization, all worked to create an explosive situation: anything seemed possible, especially given that the majority of the Socialist Party (PSI) was 'maximalist', i.e. revolutionary, refusing to participate in any bourgeois government. The first factory occupations occurred in March 1919, at Bergamo, where a factory committee took control of production.[23] By the end of 1919 a network of councils in the Piedmontese metal industry involved 150,000 workers. A general strike broke out in Turin in April 1920 concerning legal time (introduced during the war, and which the employers were anxious to suppress). In fact, the strike rapidly turned political, the employers proving exceptionally intransigent and refusing to recognize a non-union workers' delegation. The movement also met with the resistance of the metalworkers' federation, the FIOM, which was hostile to the factory committees. With the PSI refusing to call for an extension of the strike to Italy as a whole, the dispute ended in a compromise that was far from satisfactory for the Turin metalworkers.

The September 1920 strike, on the other hand, broke out in Milan and affected the whole of Italy. Virtually everywhere it was accompanied by factory occupations and even workers' control. But this time the strike had been called by the FIOM as a tactical weapon aimed at breaking the employers' lock-out; it was certainly not a spontaneous and autonomous movement.[24] This strike too ended in capitulation: the promised legislation on 'workers' control' never saw the light of day.

Nevertheless, the phenomenon of rank-and-file organization had been stronger and more widespread in Italy than anywhere else. True, the climate reigning in the country was explosive, the particularly precocious development of fascism being a good indication of the closeness of social revolution. It was in the climate of revolutionary fever reigning in Turin early in 1919 that some young 'intransigent' socialists, active on the extreme left of the PSI, founded a review called *Ordine Nuovo*. The editorial committee included the future leaders of the Italian Communist Party: Togliatti, Tasca, Terracini, Gramsci. It is to the last of these that we owe an overall view of the problem of the workers' councils. Gramsci draws his inspiration from the modes of workers' representation which arose during the war, when it became quite common for workers' delegates to be elected for the purpose of maintaining discipline on the shop floor. This practice continued after the war, but was not officially recognized until February 1919, when 'internal commissions' were set up in order to supervise the fair application of the agreement which had just been signed by the FIOM and the employers regarding the Piedmontese metal-workers.[25]

Antonio Gramsci perceived the possibility of turning these commissions into workers' councils, i.e. into organizations elected by the entire rank-and-file (even non-unionized) and whose competence would not be limited solely to questions of wages, working hours and conditions.[26] He dealt with the problem of proletarian institutions since 1918, drawing lessons from the Russian Revolution, the English shop stewards' movement as well as from the ideas of the American socialist, Daniel De Leon. But his conern for the renewal of forms of class struggle is founded upon a preliminary critique of the unions which, he wrote, had developed into an unwieldy apparatus living by laws of its own, alien to the worker and external to the masses. The unions typified a period in which capital was dominant, they had become charged with a function inherent in a regime based on private property since they sold the labour force under commercial conditions in a competitive market. They were incapable of serving as an instrument in the radical renewal of society.[27]

Gramsci thought that the party too was unsuited to the new forms of proletarian struggle: existing in the political arena, it played the same role as the unions in the economic sphere, namely that of a competitive institution owing its existence to the bourgeois State. Parties and unions were no more than the agents (*agenti*) of the proletariat, to serve as instruments of impulsion (*propulsione*) of the revolutionary process.[28]

The modern form of struggle, Gramsci continued, was incarnated in the workers' councils. Their superiority over other structures stemmed from the fact that they assembled workers at their place of work, and in their capacity as producers, and not, as was the case with the unions, in their role as wage-earners. The councils stood for the negation of industrial legality: their 'revolutionary spontaneity' implied they were ready to declare class war at any moment.[29]

But the councils were not merely instruments of struggle. In the new society they were to take the place of the capitalists and assume all the functions of management and administration. Furthermore, their task would also be to improve the conditions of production as well as to increase output.[30]

Although close to the thinking of the German councillists on certain points, Gramsci's conception was not without a certain ambiguity. Unlike the Germans, Gramsci did not break completely with classical socialism, which held that party and unions were invested with the revolutionary task. Thus, following the failures of the strikes in April and September 1920, he declared, disappointed, that it was the party's task (a regenerated and reorganized party, it is true) to give the signal for the revolution, and not that for a strikers' rally. One should not exaggerate his criticisms of the party: the target for his fury was the historical PSI, but he never questioned the superiority of *separate* political action.[31] He constantly assigned the socialists the task of conquering the majority inside the councils, and this majority was to play an active role in the revolution.[32] Finally, far from denying the role of the unions, he recognized that they played a useful function of education and preparation for the class struggle.[33]

Did Gramsci's 'spontaneist' period, in which he even went so far as to talk of the proletariat's 'self-liberation', result from his idealization of the Russian soviets (about which he was ill-informed)?[34] Did it come from some ephemeral libertarian influence, since militant anarchists had been active in the Turin movement?[35] At all events, from 1921 Gramsci fell in step with the Third International's doctrine concerning councils. By April of that year he was writing: 'The party is the highest form of organization; the unions and shop-floor councils are intermediary forms of organization'.[36] Henceforth, he proclaimed, the task of 'directing the spontaneity of the masses' ought no longer to fall upon the councils but upon the party, a powerfully organized and centralized, Bolshevik-type party.[37] Gramsci subsequently became leader of the young Italian Communist Party (PCI) and held high office in the Comintern; his council period was to be relegated to the bottom drawer of official communist history. In any case, his thinking on this subject was too marked with ambiguity, the audacity of his critique of the party was too illusory for him to be able to tread some marginal path, outside the orthodox communism with which he was to finish by identifying completely.

Despite similar situations of revolutionary ferment in a number of belligerent countries, it was only in Germany that a definite break with the past was made, and that we find the development of a theory of councils opposed to party communism.

From left-wing radicalism to left-wing communism

Council communism was not born along with councils themselves, although the appearance of the latter did precipitate its formulation. As a political theory it constitutes the culmination of a long tradition of radical opposition within the German social-democratic movement and the unions. The conflict with reformist tendencies is as old as socialist workers' organizations themselves. If we stick to the period following the 'laws on socialists',[38] we can see that a vigorous left-wing opposition began making itself heard within the ranks of the socialist party as early as 1890. Its spokesmen, known as the 'Young People' (*Die Junge*), protested against the bureaucratic and dictatorial atmosphere almost reigning in the party. The cult of the leader (*Führerprinzip*), they claimed, enabled an all-powerful leadership, paid by the party, to stifle any sign of revolutionary spirit and to continue to play the parliamentary game for all it was worth. Revolution had now become a slogan regularly repeated inside the Reichstag. But then, this purely parliamentary game was well-suited to the essentially reformist tastes of the leadership. The 'Young People' were excluded from the party at the Erfurt Congress (1891) and went on to found independent socialist groups. Such well-known publicists, anarchist militants and anarcho-syndicalists as Gustav Landauer and Fritz Kater were to emerge from the ranks of these independent socialists.

A similar battle was then raging within the trade union organization. An anti-authoritarian and revolutionary fraction had, since the Congress of Halberstadt (1892), been criticizing bitterly the narrow centralism and the purely reformist tactics of the leadership. The leadership's opponents demanded autonomy for local organizations (hence their nickname: 'the localists'), access to strike funds and greater initiative in the launching of industrial action for the rank-and-file sections. In 1897 they managed to set up an independent fraction where, under the influence of French revolutionary syndicalism after 1907, libertarian ideas came to predominate.

The other oppositional current began to develop in the early years of this century. Although it was Marxist, its reading of Marx and Engels was far more radical than that of social-democratic orthodoxy. *Left-wing radicalism*, while violently opposed to anarchism, had a number of points in common with it, notably its mistrust of party apparatus and its faith in the autonomous practices of the masses. Following the elimination of libertarian elements from the socialist and union organizations it was this current which took up the standard, in anticipation of post-war council communism.

There were three main currents of thought within the German

social democratic party at the turn of the century. The revisionist right, without always acknowledging its debt to Edward Bernstein, called for a policy akin to that of the left-wing bourgeois parties, similar to the French radical party or the English Liberals. Then there was the 'Marxist Centre', in control of the party, and whose authorized theoretician was Karl Kautsky. Under cover of strict doctrinal orthodoxy (contrary to the revisionists, he believed in the inevitability of revolution), Kautsky lent his authority to a markedly prudent tactic that was scarcely any different from the one Bernstein was calling for. A third family of thought emerged during the Russian Revolution of 1905–7. The left-wing radicals (*Linksradikalen*), as they were called, gathered around Rosa Luxemburg, whose book *The Mass Strike, the Political Party and the Trade Union* first appeared in 1906.[39]

Drawing inspiration from her experience of the Russian Revolution, Rosa Luxemburg put forward in this book a number of ideas which had already been in circulation for some years, notably among the Dutch Tribunists.[40] She shows that, in European Russia, revolutionary actions – strikes, revolts, street demonstrations – appeared *spontaneously*, unprovoked by any party. Russian social democracy was insufficiently established among the proletariat, with the result that the workers themselves created the revolutionary organizations the situation demanded: strike committees, factory committees, workers' councils. The radicality of their actions was unfettered by the existence of a heavily structured party or of a powerful, but soporific union. In Germany, the spontaneity of the workers was stifled by bureaucratization of the apparatus, by organization fetishism, the cult of the leader. Hundreds of permanent party and union officials went on applying their own policy, cut off from the rank-and-file, reluctant to undertake any bold initiatives for fear of jeopardizing their magnificent organizational edifice, which no longer served any useful purpose. Preservation of the means (the organization) now came to take priority over the objective (the revolution).[41]

In her dispute with Kautsky, Luxemburg held that organization was not a static phenomenon but a process: workers provide themselves with the organizational forms most appropriate to their struggle. The artificial separation of economic and political action is absent from these organizations. The party's parliamentarian policies, and the strictly wage-demand-oriented policies of the unions, are to be submerged beneath the development of spontaneous actions such as mass strikes. Tactically speaking this quarrel took on a more concrete character in the years 1908–10, when the party leadership ruled out a general strike as a means of fighting for the suppression of the plural electoral college in Prussia.

But although Rosa Luxemburg developed a theory of mass spontaneity which permitted her to stigmatize the party's immobilism and its congenital reformism, she failed to draw all the organizational and theoretical conclusions which flowed from this theory. To the end of her life she remained a militant profoundly attached to the party of the masses, to the hierarchy, to the congresses and their motions – in short, to everything which had made up the essence of pre-1914 social democracy.[42]

The Dutch, and Anton Pannekoek in particular, did draw all the conclusions, and notably the organizational ones, from their radical critique of Kautskyite socialism. Their discussion of the general strike took place rather earlier, in 1903, and their attacks on the reformism of the SDAPH (Social Democratic Workers' Party of Holland) led them to break away and found a new party (the SDP, Social Democratic Party) in 1909. This party never attracted more than a few hundred activists and it stayed outside the Second International (which didn't want it anyway), but this break did illustrate the extent of the divergences between Gorter, Pannekoek and Roland-Holst on the one hand, and Troelstra, who was a faithful follower of Kautsky, on the other.[43]

The Tribunists' major criticism of Troelstra and his Dutch followers concerned their entirely mechanistic conception of Marxism. While it is true that the proletariat's importance derives from its place and its function in the productive process, said Pannekoek, one should not imagine that the outbreak of revolution is inevitable. Similarly, organization is important for the simple reason that it renders the masses strong, disciplined, fusing the will of each and everyone into a single will. True, parliamentarianism is a powerful means of increasing the cohesion of the working class. And alongside this, syndicalism is necessary in order to arouse workers to fight and induce them to accept class discipline. But, Pannekoek points out, 'socialism will not come about merely because all men finally admit its superiority over capitalism and its aberrations'.[44] The working class must, in addition, be *conscious* of the necessity of the struggle and of socialism. Pannekoek thought this subjective factor was extremely important, while Kautsky ignored it. Class consciousness, the former held, is acquired through engagement in mass action, led by the workers themselves. Parliamentarianism on the other hand, which was the leadership's essential activity, is not the class struggle. Certainly in the past it made it possible to unify the proletariat, but it could never lead to socialism. As for the unions, they are an institution by now perfectly integrated into the capitalist system, since their function is to sell the labour force.

This critique led Pannekoek to relativize the role of the party and the unions, without, however, going so far as to examine them from the viewpoint of historically situated and dated organizational forms. In his quarrel with Kautsky between 1911 and 1913, on the other hand, he denies the possibility of transforming the existing State into a socialist State by means of an electoral majority, and he declares that the bourgeois State will have to be destroyed utterly (*vernichtet*), its power annihilated (*aufgelöst*).[45]

But this revolution cannot be accomplished peacefully; it will not be brought about by the present leaders' prudent policies. It will require all the might and the will of the proletariat in action. Parliamentarianism and union demands are no longer enough. New forms of capitalism (monopolies, cartels, the internationalization of production and markets) have given rise to new forms of struggle: mass actions. The passive attitude of the 'marxist centre' stems from its fear that, by 'ill-considered' initiatives, the masses will destroy their patiently constructed organizations. The chiefs, with Kautsky at their head, saw their role as that of brake, a check on 'wildcat' initiatives. For Pannekoek, this was a singularly restricted conception of organization, lingering over its external forms, its visible structures. And this at a time when the emergence of an economy based on large units had aroused in the proletariat a feeling of common belonging (*Zusammengehörigkeit*): it is this spiritual factor which leads men to organize, to develop structures. One may throw over external forms, the subjective element is indestructible.[46]

On the eve of the war, the Dutch Marxists had thus gone a long way towards an organizational and theoretical break with the Second International. They had demonstrated the limited character of parliamentary struggle (without, however, entirely rejecting it as yet), the capitalist essence of unions (whose usefulness they nevertheless continued to underline), and had made the destruction of political power the number-one task of the revolutionary movement. Finally (together with the Bulgarians and the Russians, it is true), they had shown it was possible to break with the social-democratic movement. But above all, they drew lasting lessons as to the relativity of the forms the class struggle was capable of assuming, from the mass movements of recent years (1893, 1903, 1905–7, 1908, 1910). It was quite natural, then, that they should adopt the new organizational structures which were to emerge during and immediately after the First World War.

The war precipitated the latent tendencies in left-wing radical-

ism. What had started out as a simple critique of orthodox socialism was to develop into both a social movement and a revolutionary theory in its own right.

Two kinds of factor worked in favour of this. On the one hand,
the war had brought to a head German social democracy's desire
(but the same phenomenon had occurred at the same moment in
the other belligerent countries) for integration into bourgeois society and even (after November 1918) to perpetuate it. This was, in
fact, the underlying significance of the 'Sacred Union' (*Burgfriede*,
or 'civil peace') wherein the SPD, by its votes in favour of war
credits, its abstention from any meaningful opposition, implicitly
approved the German government's war policy. Parallel to this,
the unions, by deliberately avoiding involvement in industrial
disputes, and by even going so far as to cooperate with the military
authorities in preventing or breaking strikes which began to sim-
mer spontaneously in factories throughout the Reich from 1916 on,
had set themselves up as enemies of the workers. It very soon
became clear that it would only be possible to carry on the struggle
in spite of, and against the union leaderships. A whole section of
the German proletariat thus fell vulnerable to the ideas of the left
opposition.[47] In less than three years, this had been transformed
from a handful of intellectuals into an imposing mass movement.
By June 1917 the left opposition accounted for more than half the
membership of the union organization, and the spring 1917
breakaway showed just how far the party itself had been affected.

Theory too leaped forward, emboldened by the example of the
Russian Revolution and the appearance of councils inside the
Reich itself. The constitution of autonomous bodies, both in the
factories and in provinces and towns, was due to the causes
mentioned above. The moment the workers' leaders began fulfil-
ling the repressive functions of the employers and the police, each
movement, each strike became a revolt. Especially since the slightest action inside a factory almost automatically resulted in the
sacking of union officials, cessation of the payment of union dues
and the improvisation of temporary structures. Thus, even if to
begin with a strike was purely concerned with, say, a wage claim,
it nevertheless developed rapidly into an action in which political
and economic questions fused to undermine the social *status quo*.

Left-wing radical theory fed voraciously off these examples of
mass spontaneity. The organization of councils as the expression
of autonomous struggle became the fundamental concept of the
new radicality.

Right from the beginning of the war, left-wing militants had
sought to distinguish themselves from patriotic social democracy.

Towards the end of 1914 Rosa Luxemburg, Franz Mehring, Otto Rühle and Karl Liebknecht established a small oppositional circle, the 'Internazionale' group, later to be known as the 'Spartakus Group'. Liebknecht broke with party discipline in December 1914 by voting against military credits, and he was followed by Rühle in the spring of 1915. Their resolute opposition to the war united all left-wing radicals, with their hatred of all leaderships (*Instanzen*), parliamentary leaders, paid officials, party propagandists. But divergences soon appeared within the ranks of the extreme left. The origins of this split can be traced back to the preceding period and to the attitude adopted towards social democracy.

A right wing, for whom the Spartakist leaders acted as spokesmen,[48] had no wish to break with the party, fearing that by so doing they would 'cut themselves off from the masses'. Underlying this argument was their reluctance to break with the old organizational forms and with the old Second International habits, object of so much obloquy in the past.

This wing linked up with the centrist fraction of the party, the 'Sozialdemokratische Arbeitsgemeinschaft', in April 1917 in order to found the independent social-democratic party (USPD), which took a very moderate line, and whose organization scarcely differed from that of the SPD.

The other wing was more extremist, and followed their ideological premises right through to their conclusion. The extreme left-wing radicals were made up of local groups, independent of each other, although some of them had already been bastions of the opposition before the outbreak of war. This was the case, for example, of the Berlin group, gathered around the review *Lichtstrahlen* (edited by Julian Borchardt); the Bremen group, around the *Bremer-Bürger-Zeitung* and, subsequently, the *Arbeiterpolitik* (with Karl Radek, Paul Fröhlich, Johann Knief), which was heavily influenced by Pannekoek's thinking; the Hamburg group, which edited *Kampf*, under the direction of Heinrich Laufenberg and Fritz Wolffheim. Other extreme left-wing groups were active in Dresden, Frankfurt and Brunswick. Unlike the Spartakists, who had not entirely broken with social democracy, the extremists were hoping to individualize themselves, organizationally speaking. In their view, the task of the future for the proletariat was to construct its own organization and conduct its own policy.[49]

Although they managed to cut all their bridges (and especially the financial ones) with the party, the extremists only came together in a distinct structure in 1920. But as early as autumn 1915 they had labelled themselves 'Internationals', after the Bremen and Hamburg delegates had approved Lenin's proposal to construct the Third International at the Zimmerwald Conference (September 1915), while the Spartakists had preferred to maintain their links with the Second International.

Thus, on the eve of the Russian Revolution, the Internationals[50] were very clearly moving away from the Spartakists on two points. For one thing they were demanding an organization built along different lines from the old forms found in their entirety in the USPD. They wanted an organization arising out of the struggle itself and action-orientated (*Aktionsfähig*).[51] Secondly, in order to mark their complete estrangement from pre-war organized socialism, they planned to construct a new International. It was these ideas that Pannekeok advocated in the organ of the Zimmerwald Left, which he edited with his compatriot, Henrietta Roland-Holst.[52]

With the October Revolution in Russia, the November 1918 revolution in Germany and the growth of factory committees and workers' councils, the Internationals had at last found a concrete form for the organization of their struggle. Soviet Russia illustrated their own notion of dictatorship of the proletariat, with power emanating from the base and rising towards the town and rural councils.[53] As a result of their enthusiasm for the Russian Revolution they altered their label, and in November the ISD (International Socialists of Germany) became the IKD (International Communists of Germany), publishing a paper called *Der Kommunist*, propagating the slogan: 'All power to the soviets'.

Paradoxically, the Russian Revolution brought the Internationals and the Spartakists together again; in view of the extent of revolutionary turbulence they decided to merge and found the German Communist Party (KPD).[54]

The constitutive congress took place in Berlin, 30–31 December 1918, in the midst of great exaltation. But this was not enough to wipe out divergences, and the antagonistic currents were to crystallize around three questions. What form of organization should dominate in the new party (centralization, or decentralization with autonomy for the local sections)? Should the new party vote for the Constituent Assembly (and thus participate in the parliamentary institutions)? Finally, what should be the party's attitude towards the unions (entry into the existing unions in order to stimulate opposition from within, or construction of new, even original organizations?).

The delegates divided into two blocs more or less along the lines separating the left and right wings of the old left-wing radicals. A right-wing minority (Rosa Luxemburg, Karl Liebknecht, Karl Radek, Paul Levi) favoured electoral participation, entry into the existing unions and a centralized, hierarchized organization. Although (through the intermediary of Radek) this group had the blessing of the Bolsheviks, it was nevertheless very attached to the *spirit* of social democracy, which it intended to perpetuate in the new party. The majority, on the other hand, emerged as the heirs to the boldest themes of left-wing radicalism. It contained most of the extremist groups (the Bremen, Hamburg, Dresden, etc., Internationals) and the left wing of the Spartakists which, for the first time, came out into the open to express its disagreement with the respected leaders.[55]

The confusion between Spartakists (starting with its leaders) and the revolutionary wing of the left-wing radicals was deliberately encouraged by communist historiography in subsequent years. In reality, however, the Spartakists were always rather more cautious than the Internationals, especially where tactics were concerned. It was clear right from the inaugural congress that the former intended to construct a mass party capable of playing a role in the institutional political life of the future Weimar Republic, while the latter, the Internationals, were more interested in crystallizing their thirst for revolutionary action in some completely new form of organization.

This unhappy *ménage à deux* was to last until the expulsion of the group (the majority group at that!) coming to be known as the left-wing communists (*Linkskommunisten*) at the Heidelberg Congress (October 1919).

In April 1920 the expelled group founded the KAPD (German Workers' Communist Party). Right from the start this new formation boasted 38,000 members, or rather more than half the KPD, which was left drained of life until its merger with the majority of the USPD (in December 1920), the latter bringing with it a dowry of some 300,000 militants. The party within which the left-wing communists now found themselves was supposed to incarnate the principles conceived and propagated since 1915. Its programme (inspired by Pannekoek) utterly rejected parliamentarianism and the unions. It sought to remain a party of confirmed communists working to develop the revolutionary consciousness of the masses and the struggle on the shop floor through organizations within the enterprise (*Betriebsorganisationen*). The new party was not organized along federal lines, as some might have hoped, but along the lines of 'proletarian centralism', the decisions of the highest bodies being binding.[56] Its refusal to work with the reformist unions led the KAPD to assume the programmatic leadership and long-term direction of the new factory organizations as well.

These organizations emerged during the war and their numbers increased rapidly after November 1918. They began to unite in the summer of 1919, notably in the mines and in the metalworking industries. But it was in February 1920 (*before* the creation of the KAPD) that factory committees (*Betriebsorganisationen*) came together to form the General Workers' Union of Germany (AAUD). This organization was articulated around the enterprise, the basic cell being formed by the factory or workshop; these were then organized at local, provincial (*Wirtschaftsbezirk*) and Reich levels. Its aim was to generate revolutionary agitation within the factories with a view to the destruction of capitalism and the establishment of a council republic. In 1920 the AAUD had about 100,000 members, but the following year membership declined irremediably.

The decline of council organizations (principally the AAUD, but also the anarcho-syndicalist union, the FAU) flowed from the centrifugal tendencies, apparent right from their birth, as well as from the political and social situation in the country. Factory organizations mushroomed during 1919, to the detriment of the unions, which fell back considerably, especially in the heavy industries of the Ruhr and central Germany. At first factory committees were formed spontaneously, without any precise ideological attachments. It was only towards the end of 1919 that ideological divergencies began to surface. Firstly because the communist party, under Paul Levi's leadership, was warning its militants of the dangers of 'anarchist' tendencies, inviting them to vote for the legal factory councils and not to take part in extra-union organizations. Secondly because, from December 1919 onwards, the anarcho-syndicalists, who had until then shared the views of the left-wing communists, now adopted Rudolf Rocker's anarchist-inspired programme, denying the necessity of a dictatorship of the proletariat and of the use of violence. The new programme returned to the traditional (revolutionary) syndicalist view, namely that the trade union, the instrument of economic struggle, was destined to become the fundamental organizational unit in the society of the future.

As opposed to the leaders of the KPD and the FAUD (German Free Workers' Union), the council theoreticians were thinking in terms of structures suited to both political and economic struggle, constituted at the place of work and not at the level of the locality (as in the case of the unions) or the old trade unions (the organizational base of the FAUD).

The emergence of a theory of councils coincides with that of factory organizations, though it is impossible to say which came first. At most we may presume that the example of the IWW (the

American revolutionary organization based on industrial unions) was not without influence on the thinking of the Hamburg propagandists.[57] In other words, when the AAUD was formed, only some of the factory committees actually joined it; on top of that, two tendencies began pulling the organization in opposing directions right from the first months of its existence. The Brunswick tendency, close to the left wing of the USPD, followed the IWW example, advocating the industry-wide union as the basic form of organization. It left the AAUD shortly afterwards and slid into obscurity. The other tendency, left-wing, was more deeply prejudicial to the cohesion of the *Union*. This was the so-called 'unitarist' (*Einheitsorganisationstendenz*) tendency which rejected the KAPD's control over the *Union* and demanded instead a unitary organization that would be both politically and economically oriented, bypassing political parties. This tendency was especially strong in Dresden, the fief of its chief theoretician and spokesman, Otto Rühle, who very early (in December 1920) made his section independent of the KAPD. In October 1921 his organization, the East Saxony section, led a number of other local groups out of the KAPD and founded the AAUD–E (German General Workers' League–Unitary Organization).

Aside from these centrifugal tendencies, the mass council organizations, the Leagues, were further handicapped by the overall situation in the country: inflation, growing unemployment, fiercer repression, especially since the failure of the March 1921 'action', in the course of which an embryonic insurrection was harshly stamped out by the army and the police. After 1921 the AAUD began to lose its mass character, evolving into a marginal group. It shifted away from the KAPD in 1927 and, in 1931, it formed the KAU (Communist Workers' Union) together with the remnants of the AAUD–E. As its name suggests, the KAU had no pretentions to being a mass workers' movement but consisted of a group of propagandists fighting 'to make the councils the instrument of class will'.[58]

The KAPD suffered a similarly rapid decline after 1921, torn by personal and ideological quarrels. The principal disagreements concerned the binding nature of the decisions of the highest bodies, relations with the AAUD and the question of membership of the Third International. Local groups were becoming less and less autonomous, while centralism was gradually gaining the upper hand over federalist principles, and the AAUD rapidly became a union appendix to a party congratulating itself on having brought together the 'avant-garde elements'. One final question of practical importance exacerbated the party's already considerable difficulties: should militants take part in purely economic struggles (*Lohnkampf*)? The Berlin leadership, dominated by Karl Schröder (backed up on doctrinal terrain by the Dutchman Herman Gorter), was exhibiting some singularly dictatorial and dogmatic tendencies. In March 1922 Schröder was outvoted and expelled from the party. So he formed his own 'Essen Tendency' (*Essener Richtung*), with its own paper, its own congress and its 'own' AAUD. Consequently from 1922 onwards two KAPDs coexisted alongside each other, but their numbers were derisory, with 12,000 militants in the Berlin tendency at the end of 1922, and only 600 in the Essen wing.[59]

To begin with, most of the Essen tendency's activities were taken up with the establishment of a Fourth International. This attempt in itself would only be of passing interest had it not followed immediately upon the heels of the KAPD's imbroglio with the Third International, which had caused something of a stir within the International and which marked the emergence of a communist theory of councils as opposed to the Comintern's party communism.

Council communism and party communism

We have seen that left-wing communism as it emerged in 1918 follows in the footsteps of the left-wing radicalism of the preceding period. The Bolsheviks belonged to this radical opposition in the Second International. They even (like the Dutch in 1909) went as far as breaking organizationally with Russian social democracy in 1903. Throughout the war, and more especially after the October Revolution, the Bolshevik leaders remained very close to the German extreme left, especially the Bremen Group. Both Bolsheviks and German 'Internationals' found themselves in the Zimmerwaldian Left (though not the Spartakists, who were opposed to the construction of a new international) entrusting Pannekoek and Roland-Holst with editing its official organ, *Vorbote*.[60]

The Russian Revolution was enthusiastically welcomed by all radical socialists, and especially by the Internationals, who saw in it the establishment of the dictatorship of the proletariat through the councils.[61] Their enthusiasm was all the greater in that Lenin's recent pamphlet, *State and Revolution* (published in Russia in 1918), explicitly adopted the ideas Pannekoek had expressed in his dispute with Kautsky over the destruction of the bourgeois State and of political power as such. The future left-wing communists saw in it a charter for their own revolutionary aspirations; Lenin had formulated the classic themes of the *Linksradikalen*: destruction of the State, rejection of elections (and hence of parliamentarianism), the advent of a free and equal association of producers.[62] True, closer reading of the pamphlet reveals some rather different propositions. For Lenin stated also that there would still be a (transitory) State in the post-revolutionary period, exercising an *extremely rigorous* control and, like all States, repressive.[63]

Divergences only became public in the course of 1919, when the left-wing communists (now in the KPD) realized that Moscow, and shortly afterwards the Third International, were backing the right wing of the party, in other words those elements which favoured the worst deviations of social democracy: the cult of organization for organization's sake, parliamentarianism, unionism, leader-worship. Following the assassination of its historic leaders (Luxemburg, Liebknecht, Jogiches), the 'rightist' Levi took over the party leadership (at the end of April 1919) and imposed a policy of 'entryism' into the unions, of electoral participation, by way of a stream of decisions without appeal and congresses meeting under irregular conditions.[64] Opponents were qualified pell-mell as anarchists and anarcho-syndicalists and, at the Heidelberg congress in October 1919, Levi announced that all those who disagreed with his views should leave the party, and he actually gained a majority in favour of expelling . . . the majority! And that at a time when the unions had been utterly discredited, when workers' leagues were springing up all over the country, when more and more workers were boycotting elections in favour of direct action.

In autumn 1919 the left-wing communists came round to the view that Levi was becoming increasingly tempted by social-democratic opportunism and that they, the expelled group, were the true representatives of revolutionary communism. They consequently formed their own, new communist party, whose place they thought was in the Third International. Their desire to join the new organization which Moscow had just created resulted from something of a misunderstanding. They were convinced Lenin would recognize them as communists as soon as he had a moment to talk it out with them and let himself be persuaded of the KPD's opportunism.

Unfortunately for them, the KPD's opportunism only existed because it corresponded to the policy of the new international, hence to Moscow's policy. Right from the KPD's inaugural congress Radek had come out wholeheartedly in favour of the right wing, and it was through his auspices that Levi took over the party leadership. Lenin himself, in a letter to the left-wing communists dated September 1919, had warned against non-participation in elections, and against the boycotting of unions and legal factory committees, and had described their attitude as 'an infantile disorder'.[65] He was even more incisive in his famous pamphlet on 'left-wing communism' written in spring 1920 and handed to delegates at the Second Congress of the Communist International, abandoning his earlier equivocal stance and explicitly condemning the 'Dutch leftists'. He advocated a disciplined, centralized party, taking very little notice of the federalist line favoured by the majority of German communists. Within the unions, he distinguished between leaders and masses, only the former being corrupt; from this he concluded that entry into the unions was necessary in order to win over the masses and dislodge the leadership. Similarly, he insisted upon the absolute necessity of participation in bourgeois parliaments insofar as the masses were still attached to them, and in all other bourgeois institutions capable of being entered. The parliamentary game must be exploited in all its forms: electoral alliances, compromises, collaboration. This policy being justified, in Lenin's view, by the overriding need to raise the consciousness of the masses at all costs, and to prepare the way for the soviets. The revolution needs a mass party and, in Western countries, quantity must take precedence over quality.[66]

Despite the ideological gap existing between Moscow and the left-wing communists from the outset, the latter waited two whole years before giving up hope and leaving the Third International. The KAPD sent three successive delegations to Moscow, two in the course of the summer of 1920, and one in the autumn. Otto Rühle, who travelled there in May, came back disenchanted, talking about the centralized system and the dictatorship of the party.[67] He broke with the KAPD on his return, taking with him the East Saxony region. The Party leadership was unconvinced by his report and three of the leaders, among them Gorter and Schröder, went to Moscow to see for themselves in November 1920.

Meanwhile, the Second Congress of the Communist International had just condemned 'left-wing communism' by refusing to accept the KAPD. The party's line on parliament and the unions was judged 'inadequate'. Its programme was described as 'capitulating to [revolutionary] syndicalist opinion'.[68] Furthermore, points 9 and 11 (relating to work inside the unions and in parliament) of the twenty-one conditions of admission approved at the same congress clearly contradicted the KAPD programme.

Gorter, who was determined to organize a revolutionary opposition inside the Communist International, nevertheless managed to obtain temporary admission as a 'sympathizing

party', with consultative status.[69] But Gorter's plans came to
nothing, and after the Third Communist International Congress
(summer 1921) the KAPD was ordered to merge with the KPD. It
was the end of an illusion, and henceforth Gorter and the Essen
tendency devoted themselves to setting up a Fourth International.
This, the KAI (the Communist Workers' International), was
founded in 1922 and only existed on paper, attracting a few
hundred militants, mostly German and Dutch.[70]

Despite these organizational avatars, from the middle of 1920
onwards, council theory was no longer merely the most extreme
expression of left-wing radicalism, but had emerged as being
diametrically opposed to Bolshevik ideology as shared by those
communist parties which had subscribed to the conditions
imposed by the Comintern. From this moment on we can begin to
speak of a *council communism*, carrying on the radical tradition of
Marxism and opposed to *party communism*, heir to the opportunism of the Second International.

Consequently, council theory originally posed as a virulent
critique of the very party which was to be known later on as the
'orthodox' or 'official' communist party, and which eventually
became the 'Marxist–Leninist' party. In place of unions and
parties, council communism proposes natural, i.e. historical,
groupings of the masses: the councils. Finally, it replaced the
Russian Revolution in the context of the historical evolution of
capitalism by looking upon it as a bourgeois revolution.

Parliamentarianism, party and unions, the councillists claimed,
are forms of struggle adapted to another, pre-revolutionary, age.
During this historical phase, which ended more or less with the
First World War, the proletariat was not very numerous and was
utterly atomized. It needed an organization to defend its immediate interests, leaders to represent it in the institutions of the
bourgeois State. In that period the unions undeniably played a
positive role, extracting from the capitalists concessions indispensable to the improvement of workers' well-being. Similarly,
the socialist parties unified the class, which thus found itself indi-
vidualized and represented *en bloc*.[71] But, rapidly, as the workers
grew in numbers, these organizations external to the working class
began generating their own bureaucracy, which made itself
increasingly independent of the masses and tended to defend its
own interests. As a result, the organizations started to identify
with the capitalist system and hence to obstruct the revolutionary
struggle.[72]

While the proletariat was naturally reformist in the pre-First
World War period, in the following phase it aspired to revolution.

It was no longer concerned with obtaining concessions from employers or the State, but with the suppression of both. Given this objective, which is inherent in the proletariat, the old organizations and the old tactics (those of the old social-democratic movement) had become a brake upon the development of new forms of action which are essentially *mass actions*.[73]

No doubt, the left-wing radicals had demonstrated the shortcomings of parliamentarianism at any price before the war, pointing to the way it was practised by the socialist chiefs. But they did admit that it had a certain utility in the education of the masses and as a propaganda instrument. The International Socialists (ISD) themselves continued to express this view right up to the eve of the Russian Revolution.[74] As for the Dutch Marxists, they had very early on refused to assimilate the notion of parliamentary struggle to that of revolutionary struggle.[75] But no-one could possibly harbour the illusion after social democracy had behaved as capitalism's saviour in November 1918 and after. Otto Rühle even went so far as to consider that a party was incapable, by definition, of being anything other than a bourgeois institution; the term 'revolutionary party' seemed to him to be a nonsense.[76]

The unions fulfilled the same function of compromise in the economic domain as the parties on the political scene. They are merely an institution functioning within the framework of bourgeois society and, as the war had so strikingly shown, they act as a powerful shield for it. So it would be utterly absurd to think of turning the unions into revolutionary instruments. As 'organs of capital', the unions aspired to nothing more than recognition by the ruling apparatus.[77] The very development of trade unionism necessarily leads it into conflict with the working class, and the revolutionary struggle begins the moment workers decide to organize themselves outside union structures. The union leaders cling to their positions and to their new social status (for their union role has turned these former workers into petit bourgeois), summoning up all their strength in order to oppose the revolution and communism.[78]

The Third International leadership had imposed the conception of a mass communist party on communists in the West. As a result of this they everywhere encouraged the unification of revolutionary minorities with the left wing of social democracy. Thus, the KPD was transformed overnight from a group of a few thousand members into a powerful party with more than 300,000 members. The council communists attacked this tactic which, in their view, could only bring about a situation where the leaders dominated. For the great majority of these newcomers were far from having attained a communist consciousness, and this could only mean that they would hand over responsibility to their leaders. Under these conditions, the revolution could lead only to a party, but not to a class dictatorship. When a class is not yet ready for revolution, no-one can carry it through in its place. And when a minority seizes power and holds on to it in the name of the proletariat, it is merely following a neo-Blanquist line, not communism. It is important to deliver the workers not only from their physical and material subjection to the bourgeoisie, but also from their spiritual enslavement. But this immense and difficult task cannot be undertaken by some resolute avant-garde.[79] The proletarian revolution will be the work of the masses as a whole, and if they allow a party to take power in their place then all that will have been achieved is a bourgeois revolution. For the revolt against capital is also a revolt against all the old organizational forms.[80]

This brings us to the heart of council theory. The councils were not simply new forms of organization arisen to replace the old. They were also the expression of the class locked in struggle.[81] In this new phase of the struggle the proletariat was seeking to destroy the State and wage labour. It had come to realize that a revolution does not consist of a change of majority in parliament or in the fact of a political party coming to power. New forms of production, large economic units, the internationalization of markets and the development of monopolies had brought about a transformation of the worker's mentality. He now wanted to be master of his own fate and, first and foremost, of the basis of all societies: the means of production. But, although the working class already possessed the necessary material strength (numbers, but also its productive function) to overthrow its masters, it was still too impregnated with bourgeois ideology to have a clear conscience about it.[82] In consequence, the proletarian revolution was to take an entire epoch, resulting from a slow process of ripening among the masses, from an ever-growing consciousness of the tasks awaiting it.

Obviously, in this new phase of the struggle the proletariat cannot hope to rely on its old organizations now allied with capitalism. They were suited to a form of struggle in which leaders held sway over passive masses; in which revolution was conceived as an operation that had been foreseen and planned for in advance – by the leadership. The proletarian revolution, conversely, was to be the fruit of a *spontaneous* struggle waged by the class as a whole. New, more appropriate forms of organization would spring forth. But there was no need to invent them, for they already possessed a concrete historical existence: the workers' councils.[83]

Admittedly,, the emergence of these councils was not followed by the advent of a communist society. The backward economic conditions of Russia in 1917 had prevented the working class from coming to power. It could have happened in Germany in November 1918, if the workers had not been halted in their tracks by the conceptions which social democracy had been inculcating in them for years. These historical examples at least proved that the time for mass action had arrived, that communism would be established by the councils.[84]

The fact that the councils only had a very limited historical existence (in Russia they rapidly became State organs, the docile instruments of party domination) leads one to wonder whether the council communists restricted their role to the pre-revolutionary period or not. The answers to this question are not really very uniform. Most theoreticians, however, attribute a double function to them, seeing in them both a revolutionary organization *and* the basis of future communist society. That is, they are supposed to act both as a unit for struggle and destruction in the revolutionary period, and as wielders of economic (above all, the management of production) and political (dictatorship of the proletariat) powers in the subsequent phase.[85] But while all are agreed on this, some go on to assign the proletariat the task of forming councils right away, while others see councils merely as the organs of a future council State.[86]

As long as we stick to the critique of party communism and to the role of councils in the revolutionary process and in communism's transitional phase, most members of the council movement are more or less in agreement. Differences arise when one tries to answer the age-old question of the *present* organization of revolutionaries. The advent of a network of councils would signal a very advanced stage of class consciousness: by assuming responsibility for the abolition of profit-based society themselves, the workers would thereby demonstrate that they had acquired a genuinely communist mentality. Until then, those with a clear awareness of the tasks, the communists, constituted a minority. Should they organize themselves, should they intervene in the workers' struggles to show them the way ahead? Then, if they were to come together in a joint organization, what sort of structure should this have?

All these questions gave rise to heated debate in councillist circles and continue to divide them to this day. Schematically, we can say that the great majority of council communists are opposed to the idea of any external group *directing* the struggle inside factories. Similarly, in principle, the council movement is hostile to the party communists' views on centralism, discipline and hier-archy. That said, in fact one finds nuances covering all colours of the spectrum bounded by two poles, the one tending towards organization, the other towards spontaneity.

At the time when council communism was incarnated in a genuine movement, roughly during the 1920s, there was a great temptation to construct a councillist *party*. This tendency was represented by the KAPD leaders, and especially their theoreti-cian, Herman Gorter. Gorter (1864–1927) was one of the great Dutch poets of the impressionist school. He began to play an active role in the SDAP (Dutch Social Democratic Party) from 1896, opposing the revisionist tendency. After 1907 he joined the oppositional group which was to found the tiny Socialist Party (SDP) in 1909 (with Pannekoek, Van Ravesteyn and Wynkoop). In 1918 he took part in the foundation of the Dutch communist party, before travelling to Germany, where he joined the left wing of the KPD. From 1920 on he became the theoretician of both the German KAP (Essen tendency) and its Dutch counterpart, which he man-aged to bring together to form a Communist Workers' Interna-tional (KAI) in 1922.[87]

In Gorter's view the proletariat needed two kinds of organiza-tion: those based on the place of work, the factory, and those bringing 'enlightened' militants together. The former would con-stitute workers' leagues while the others would form the party. The workers' league is a mass organization concerned with every-day struggle in the factory. But the drawback of the league is its tendency to reformism, confining itself to wage claims. Or, con-versely, as a result of an erroneous evaluation of the situation, it is liable to utopianism. The party, on the other hand, is there to steady the helm: it is capable of pointing the way ahead since it is composed of that fraction (however minimal) of the work-ing class which possesses the knowledge and a clear conscious-ness of the revolutionary objectives. The Western proletariat needed these 'pure' parties, reminders of the one formed by the Bolsheviks in 1902–3. But the party must not seek to gain power for its own ends, for the revolutionary dictatorship is to be that of the entire class. In any case, Gorter prophesied, the proletariat of the industrialized countries of Western Europe and North America is far too numerous for a dictatorship of the party to be possible. The party of pure communists prefigures the political councils, while the unions anticipate the advent of economic councils.[88]

Gorter's organizational conceptions were not all that different from Lenin's own; a party–union duality, with the former taking precedence over the latter had after all been set forth in *What is to be Done?* as early as 1902.

Nor did Otto Rühle (1874–1943) entirely abandon this line, except insofar as he advocated a 'unitary' organization. Rühle had been a teacher with a deep interest in pedagogic and psychological problems as well as a social-democrat deputy in the Reichstag when the war broke out. He followed Liebknecht in voting against the war credits in March 1915. Right from the foundation of the KPD he found himself in the left-wing opposition, which he subsequently followed into the KAPD, taking with him his own organization in East Saxony (he had been elected President of the Dresden workers' council in November 1918). On his return, disappointed, from a trip to Soviet Russia he separated his regional group from the KAPD and, in 1921, realized his project of creating a unitary organization with the foundation of the AAU–E. [89] This incarnated Rühle's underlying belief that the organization of the revolutionary vanguard (which he considered indispensable) should not take the form of a political party. It was in the enterprise that the primary battlefield in the struggle against the power of capital was to be found, and it was on this basis that conscious revolutionaries would seek to unite. The BO (workers' organizations) federated and gradually formed the Unitary Workers' League (AAU–E). This League took on the characteristics of revolutionary struggle – economic and political – and concerned itself with both. It was governed by the federalist principle: no centralism, no leadership 'from outside', no interference by intellectuals not belonging to the plant. Delegates could be revoked at any time, while the leaders were no more than spokesmen for the rank and file, its executive organs. The task of unitary organization consisted of developing class consciousness and a feeling of solidarity among workers. Neither a party nor a union, the AAU–E was the revolutionary organization of the proletariat. It dissolved itself with the appearance of the councils which, in some ways, it had prefigured. [90]

The intermediate conception, halfway between the 'organizationalists' and the 'spontaneists', was developed by Pannekoek, arising logically from his views on the nature of the revolutionary struggle, which he tied directly to class consciousness. Anton Pannekoek (1873–1960) was an astronomer of world-renown and an historian of science; throughout his life he pursued a dual career as militant and scientist. He was active in the socialist movement for over half a century. He joined the Dutch SDAP in 1902 and, in the following year, began developing his theory of mass spontaneity. He was invited to Berlin in 1905 in order to teach at the party school, and henceforth he became active in both organizations. He became involved in the Bremen left-wing radical circles from 1906 onwards, contributing a large number of articles to the party journals. He was expelled from Germany in 1914 on account of his Dutch nationality, but he carried on his activities in Switzerland and Holland within the Zimmerwaldian left while keeping up his contacts with the German international socialists. He withdrew from active militant work after 1921 to devote himself to astronomy, which he taught at the University of Amsterdam from 1925 onwards. He nevertheless contributed to the theoretical work of the Dutch council communists, the GIC (International Communists Group), and published numerous articles in various council-communist reviews in the 1930s and 40s.

Pannekoek insisted with greater force than his companions upon the spiritual aspect of the class struggle. Certainly, he remained a convinced Marxist and materialist. But in his view material factors (relations of production) had no immediate influence upon the revolutionary process. The timelag between the emergence of new material structures or new modes of production and the moment the worker's consciousness becomes aware of them and adapts to them may be very long. Meanwhile, the worker's consciousness remains the prisoner of the beliefs, prejudices and false values of the surrounding culture. The power of the bourgeoisie is spiritual before all else: the bourgeoisie controls religion, education, propaganda activities and, more generally, the entire range of cultural production, to which the worker is more or less subjected. There is thus a gap between the material situation as it is today, and collective consciousness. Hence the need to raise the proletariat's consciousness of its emancipatory tasks, while it is growing in numbers and while its role in the productive process makes it the true master of this process.[91]

If it is to be carried through to its conclusion, the revolution must first exist in the consciousness of the proletariat. The latter will find its own road to freedom through its struggles. But at the same time it is vital to develop and broaden its consciousness. And this is where the communists, those who have reflected and who have mastered the science of historical evolution, find their role. These enlightened elements are to meet in small groups which Pannekoek saw as being external to the scene of the practical struggle, namely the enterprise. Theirs is a function of clarification, explanation and discussion. It is their duty constantly to render the task to be accomplished ever more clearcut and evident; their task is tirelessly to propagate, in their writings and in their speeches, ideas and knowledge, formulating objectives, enlightening the masses. Just as the workers' councils constitute the units of practical action in the class struggle, these discussion groups represent its spiritual force.[92]

The precise outlines of these groups, which Pannekoek sometimes called parties, remain vague. They are without status, nor do they have membership cards or regular subscriptions. Most important, it is not their job to direct conflicts. It does not really matter to him what they are called so long as they are different from what we normally know as parties. These groups bring together all those who share the same underlying conceptions in order to discuss and to discover the tasks to be accomplished. Their activities are purely intellectual, and their importance stems from the fact that victory will ultimately depend upon the spiritual force of the proletariat as well.[93]

Alongside Pannekoek's rather moderate positions (his ideas concerning the party consisted of nuances), some council communists' views were rather more blunt, rejecting all forms of 'external' organization, no matter what its profile might be.

During the period 1917–23 one encounters conceptions which more closely resemble certain anarchist tendencies than the prevailing Marxism. As early as 1917, Julian Borchardt, for example, stated that all parties were alike and proclaimed the right to autonomy in the face of all authority, even that derived from the revolutionary party. Borchardt even rejected the form of the party itself, retaining only its 'executive organs' (*Ausführende Organe*).[94] A little later a fraction developed inside the 'unitarist' branch of the council communists (AAU–E) demanding the dissolution of all general organizational structures (i.e. ones bringing together rank-and-file groups).[95] But these two tendencies stood at the outer edges of council theory. On the other hand, a certain number of councillists put forward ideas in the 1930s derived by strict interpretation from the very heart of this theory. For these people, it was impossible to distinguish between the class struggle and the acts of the workers; the workers' movement coincided with the movement of the workers. It is governed by its own laws tending toward the appropriation of the means of production. Not only does it create its own organs of material struggle (factory or action committees) but also its own organs of intellectual knowledge: working groups. These groups are no longer gatherings of individuals external to the class but constitute an instrument forged by the class itself and within its own ranks. This will lead to the autonomous organization of the masses into councils, and the autonomous organization of *revolutionary workers* into working groups.[96] In other words, all intervention from outside is eliminated; all efforts in the direction of the final objective must come from within the class and any exception to this can only be inspired by the 'ex-workers' movement.

We have seen how council theory broke away from left-wing radicalism, establishing its own individuality *against* the conceptions Moscow was propagating through the Third International. With the passing years, the question of the Russian Revolution, its nature and characteristics, was to take an increasingly important place in the discussions of these 'working groups'. The councillists developed not one but two successive conceptions of the Russian Revolution, the content of these conceptions being inseparable from their theory as a whole.

To begin with, from 1919 on, radical theoreticians accepted that Russia had undergone a true revolution, abolishing the old regime and carrying the proletariat to power. But the specific conditions predominating in this backward country meant that the revolution could not be expected to assume the same forms as those it would surely take on in the industrialized countries of western Europe and North America. For these countries possessed large, educated proletariats, with long histories behind them; they could not rely upon other social categories for the completion of their historical task. In Germany, for example, the mass of peasants was composed of tenant farmers and smallholders whose sole ambition was to enlarge and protect their property: they were the natural allies of the industrial bourgeoisie. The proletariat could only count on its own forces, material and spiritual. The day it arose, it would take upon itself the destruction of the old structures and, above all, it would exercise its own dictatorship – class dictatorship. In Russia, on the other hand, six million workers had been backed by a vast mass of peasants also aspiring to the expropriation of the capitalists. Once it had achieved power, however, this numerically weak working class (in a country of 180 million inhabitants), devoid of any tradition of freedom or class consciousness, was obliged to yield power to a party made up of conscious and devoted communists whose policy could not ignore the social base of its regime: the peasantry. Which explains why the dictatorship which was in fact exercised was not one of a class but that of a party, a bureaucracy, or more likely that of a few leaders only.[97]

In spite of this analysis, or perhaps because of it, the council communists identified themselves with the Russian Revolution and did not question the rightness of Bolshevik theory and practice. Bolshevik tactics were considered perfectly appropriate to the situation of an economically backward country; all they asked of

the CPSU was that it desist from calling for the mechanical application of similar tactics to Western Europe, where the situation was
utterly different.[98]

Opinions began to evolve from about 1921–2, when the Russian
Revolution started to emerge as a bourgeois revolution. This
change coincided with Lenin's introduction of the NEP and his
encouragement of private property, especially in the countryside.
Rühle was one of the first to demythologize the 'communist'
character of the Russian Revolution. On his return from Russia he
stated that the councils merely masked the dictatorship of the
party, and that he found no trace of genuine communism; conversely, he went on, there was a flourishing new soviet
bourgeoisie![99] Shortly afterwards all the councillists came round to
the view that what had occurred in Russia had been a democratic–bourgeois or peasant–bourgeois revolution: so far were internal policy (the restoration of private property) and external policy
(commercial and diplomatic relations with the capitalist powers)
both supposed to bear witness to a process in which power was
gradually passing into the hands of a minority and which was
leading straight towards 'State capitalism'. The tasks facing the
Russian revolutionaries were those of a defaulting bourgeoisie: the
Revolution had been made by a handful of representatives of the
petit bourgeoisie – the Bolsheviks – who had then gone on to set
themselves up as an obstacle to the world proletarian revolution.
As usual, it was Rühle who stated this idea most incisively: for
him, the more or less proletarian character of the Russian Revolution did nothing to alter its bourgeois essence in a country where
the first task was to progress from feudalism to the industrial
capitalism of the modern era. Right from the outset, he claimed,
the regime had shown itself to be bourgeois: one had only to look
to the Brest–Litovsk Treaty, the acceptance of the principle of the
right to self-determination of peoples, the persistence of private
property among the peasantry or the policy of nationalization,
which had nothing whatever to do with *socialization*.[100]

The essence of this analysis was to remain the same, even after
the forced collectivization of 1928–30, although refinements were
added later. Pannekoek later explained that the occupation of
power by the party was due to a 'shortage of cadres' and that the
State had substituted itself for the class. For him, State capitalism
was equally a form of *State socialism* since the State, in Russia, was
the sole master. With the bureaucracy carrying out tasks which, in
Western Europe, would have been those of the bourgeoisie, it was
clearly the job of the bureaucrats to impose industrialization and
the collectivization of land. This is why, despite its bourgeois

character, or rather because of it, the Russian Revolution represented an enormous step forward, the masses having advanced
from a stage of unevolving barbarianism to a situation in which
they might aspire to dignity. But the price of this progress was a
heavy one: an oppressive dictatorship, and an even more crushing
slavery than that weighing upon the working class in Western
capitalist societies.[101]

The Second World War led to no notable changes in the council
theory; a certain number of theses were accentuated, while others
were played down. The main target of struggles was now the
State–unions coalition, as a result of which new forms of conflict
were to be envisaged, such as wildcat strikes and factory occupations. These new methods (not entirely new, since the councillists
had already observed their appearance before the war) seemed to
them characteristic of the independence of thought and the autonomy of which the proletariat was now capable. The central problem in the post-war revolutionary process emerges as the extension of strikes. Since each wildcat strike brought the legality of the
system itself and property rights into question, the repressive
function of the union now acted as a spark liable to set the whole of
society alight. The councillists therefore placed all their hopes in
the powers of workers' solidarity and in the contagiousness of
action which, by degrees, would lead the workers to seize the
instruments of production. For nationalization alone will not do
away with exploitation: a new bureaucracy will inevitably arise, as
in the USSR, to take the place of the old exploiting class. The
radical solution is the one which leads the workers to control the
means of production for themselves.[102]

A few tiny groups propagating council theory or else theories close
to it survived in the following years in Holland, Australia, Britain
and France. Since the end of the 1960s, however, the ideas and
traditions of council communism have suddenly enjoyed a fresh
vogue. It has become one of the stars in the theoretical firmament
of the New Left.[103] This is why it is necessary to situate, or at least
to try to do so, the theses of the council movement in relation to the
aspirations of the new radicality.

There can be no doubt whatsoever that the council theorists
remain within the path traced by Marxism: their aim is to supply
the one true, undeformed interpretation of Marxian thought.
Furthermore, their Marxism is very narrowly determinist, and in
spite of the importance Pannekoek accords to the spiritual factor
and to consciousness, council communism's interpretation of historical materialism remains rather restrictive. The relations of pro-

duction are seen as modifying, with or without timelag, social life and its evolution. As Gorter stated, men may make their own history, but only within rather narrow limits. Historical evolution is contained within the transformation of the modes of production.

This determinism, rather distant from the spirit of the new radicality, all too often gives rise to a certain dogmatism. Councillists believe firmly in the crisis of capitalism inevitably resulting in the emergence of revolutionary consciousness. Even if they are a good deal less dogmatic than a Kautsky or a Lenin, the council communists are nevertheless marked by a strict economism.[104]

The other element equally foreign to contemporary revolutionary thought concerns the central place assigned to the enterprise in the process of liberation. Pannekoek tells us that production is the very essence of society and that enterprises are its constitutive cells.[105] This statement flows from his very imperative historical materialism and his excessive valorization of economic factors. This valorization accounts for the councillists' conception of work: for them, work was considered desirable, indispensable, the source of all spiritual and social life. In other words, their conception of work differed barely from the quasi-religious image presented by Marx and Engels. The worker-controlled society advocated by the councillists turns out to be an immense factory; neither the unpleasantness nor the tedium of work will have disappeared. Far from liberating man from productive work, this vision binds him to it permanently and irremediably.

Otto Rühle even went as far as to hold that the worker is only really a proletarian when inside his factory. Outside, he is a petit bourgeois, philistine in his life-style, dominated by the ideology of the dominant class. Only in his place of work does he become a revolutionary.[106] One ends up wondering just how the worker manages to sustain this split personality; can a single individual really have twin mentalities, or two faces, like Janus? This question leads us to a more fundamental critique expressing the hard core of radical theory, namely the very partial character of council communism. For the concepts of council communism only really grasp one facet of human alienation, ignoring the other aspects, including the everyday life of the individual which lies at the heart of the radical critique. It is not certain that the proletarian is better armed in the professional struggle than he is in the fight against cultural, family and sexual repression.

Even where the role (ambiguous, to say the least) of 'conscious minorities' – working groups or new-style parties – is concerned, council communism borrows rather too many elements from classical Marxism for it not to be a little suspect in the eyes of the new radicals. The councillists were of bourgeois origin for the most part, intellectuals who were well-established in careers in the surrounding society. There is something paradoxical about their enthusiasm for the messianic role of the workers – the *others*, to employ the existentialist's vocabulary – when one considers that the autonomy or the self-movement of the proletariat lies at the centre of their preoccupations.

For all this, the councillists did contribute an historical contradiction of Leninist ideology. In those dark years when the Third International stood out as the incarnation of revolutionary hopes, the councillists demystified this claim while starting from the same theoretical premises as the official communists.

Finally, by referring first and foremost to the historical experience of the councils they gave content and illustration to one of the fundamental demands of radicality, namely that the struggle for liberation from all constraints should be autonomous. And if they were not alone in placing all their hopes and faith in the experience of the councils, they nonetheless situated it within the historical evolution of radicality.

4   The critique of Marxian reification[1]

Up till now, we have considered radical thought as a critique of the substance of Marxism: of the content of Marx's ideas and, after 1917, of their realization. We have not yet looked at the critique of the form taken by Karl Marx's doctrine, namely the critique of its scientific character.

The problem immediately arises: what do we mean by 'doctrine' when dealing with a thinker who, as we know, has left his stamp upon such a wide variety of spheres, from philosophy, political science, economics and sociology (seen as the science of the laws of the evolution of society) to utopia.

For while the various shades of Marxism, from orthodoxy to left-wing extremism, disagree as to the relative importance of the different components of the total system, and while a good many view Marxian economic thought as the predominant, and even unique element, others claim to have discovered a richer, more complete 'Marx, the philosopher'. The entire critique developed by the Marxist 'philosophers' (Lukács, Korsch, the Frankfurt School, the philosophical tendency of the 1950s and 1960s) is devoted to demonstrating the importance of philosophy in the works of Marx, and the interaction between his Hegelian – or neo-Hegelian – ideas and his political, economic and sociological thought. It attempts to rehabilitate this sphere by presenting Marxism as a *totality*, claiming that social-democratic and, later, communist orthodoxy had fastened exclusively upon its economic doctrine. However, the 'philosophers' at no time challenged this doctrine itself; all they were concerned to do was to dispute the preponderance accorded to economics by the theoreticians and practitioners of Marxism, and the absurdities arrived at by reducing the latter to a form of economism.

In this sense, we may say that they managed to shake the Marxist edifice by concentrating the interest of the inquisitive Marxist upon the coherence of the parts as related to the whole and hence upon an analysis of the form of Marxism. But they never actually tackled the question of the conception of Marxian economic theory, only its results.

Paradoxically (though the paradox is only apparent), this challenge originated in the avant-garde of the arts; in twentieth-century capitalist Europe this has frequently constituted the avant-garde *tout court*. The destruction of figurative art in the period preceding the First World War, and the popularization of abstract art in the post-war period gave rise to reflection on the subject of art, its techniques and its meaning; this reflection centred around the Bauhaus, in Weimar Germany. After 1933, the spiritual heritage of the Bauhaus took refuge in Scandinavia, where there was still sufficient freedom for independent thought. Thus the Dane, V. B. Peterson, published *Symboler i abstrakt Kunst* in 1933, sparking off a wave of emulation that took root in the Movement for an Imaginist Bauhaus, of which the Danish painter and philosopher, Asger Jorn, now appears to have been the strongest personality. In 1960, Asger Jorn published a *Critique de la politique économique* ('Critique of Economic Policy'), in which he reviewed the theoretical foundations of the economic policy of Marxist socialism. His critique of socialist economic policy led him to formulate a critique of the Marxian critique of (so-called classical) political economy, and hence of *Capital*.[2] This concerns the theoretical foundations of *Capital*, and chiefly Part I, entitled: 'Commodities and Money'.

The original feature of Jorn's approach was that he did not consider the content of the critique of the capitalist economy. Instead, he chose to refute the *form* in which this critique was couched, i.e. its scientific character in the light of the concept of science as refined and developed in the twentieth century.

Reification and the Marxian critique of commodities

The word reification comes from the Latin *res* (thing, in the sense of object), and as a concept, was developed by the Marxist 'philosophers' in the 1920s, and by Georg Lukács in particular (he used the German words *Verdinglichung* and *Versachlichung*), thereby designating what Marx had meant when he used the expressions *alienation* and *the fetishism of commodities* and what Hegel had conceived of as the manifestation of alienation in the historical process.[3] Reification, for Lukács, is that phenomenon which transforms beings and thought into *things*.

Jorn gives a more precise definition of reification which, for him, is the devalorization of a concept into the status of an object. This is a consequence of the economic policy of Marxist socialism, which reduces the entire reality of the social process to its economic state, and which reduces man himself to the status of an economic factor. Jorn then turns to the Marxian critique of capitalist economics in his search for the theoretical foundations of this economic policy.

Marx viewed capitalist production as a vast accumulation of commodities, and his critique of the capitalist mode of production presupposes an analysis of commodities, which he undertakes in chapter 1 of *Capital*, the cornerstone of his entire critique. Right from the first paragraph,[4] however, Marx confuses two absolutely different notions: that of value and that of object, by identifying the one with the other. The object of utility, for Marx, becomes 'use-value', and the object of exchange (or *commodity*) 'exchange-value'. By arbitrarily identifying an object with its value, the object thereby metamorphoses into value.[5]

By confusing two distinct notions, Marx idealized the object while at the same time supplying the first example of reification of language by reducing an ideal notion, a concept, to the designation of a purely material reality. On top of this, in developing his reasoning, he arrived at an absurdity, since we cannot use a value, whereas we can and do use objects (hence the expression 'useful object'), and we do exchange goods for other goods. It is this exchange that determines price, which is the economic index of the value of a commodity.

Marx confuses these terms because he lacks a coherent philosophical conception of the world and hence of the economic phenomenon seen as a manifestation of this coherence. The absence of a philosophical system (in the Hegelian sense as set forth in the preface to *The Phenomenology of Mind*) leads him to employ the German word *Wert* in its two senses, abstract meaning value, and concrete meaning goods, product, commodity.

Asger Jorn's theory of form and the critique of commodities

In theoretical terms, the identification of value with commodity amounts to identifying *value in itself* with *the form of value*. The passage from the one to the other constitutes, as Jorn puts it, the process or substance. For *Capital* to have had a scientific value, it would have had to have been a critique of the *form of value*, that is, of commodities, and not of abstract value in itself.

The critique of form called for a theory of form, and Marx had developed no such theory.[6] Jorn proposes one that apprehends form as form of matter. He shows that matter (in the sense of raw materials) takes the form of its content, but that as soon as it is transformed, substance and form cease to coincide. When a tree is changed into a table, the material wood becomes content and the table-form becomes form. Thus, in the object of utility, matter appears as its substance : 'Forms only become substance in the process transforming them into other forms.'

Jorn generalizes from this observation to the entire economic process, and deduces a commodity cycle that is considerably more developed than the Marxian one.

In Marx, this cycle takes the form of an exchange implying the following type of changes : commodity to money to commodity or C – M – C. In this process, a commodity is exchanged for money which in turn is exchanged for a commodity. Clearly though, while this model may suffice to illustrate commercial exchange (on the market level), it is inadequate as an explanation of the total process taking place within the social economy, since it takes into account neither the stage prior to the commodity phase, nor what happens to it after the exchange. The complete cycle, according to Jorn, occurs as follows:

$$N - U - C - M - C - U - N$$

where U means useful objects and N the natural form of the objects (in the sense of raw materials).

Thus, upstream we have the transformation of nature into objects of utility and that of objects of utility into objects of exchange; downstream, we have the commodity acquired in exchange for money reverting to its use-function, i.e. utilized, and then, in the form of refuse, reintegrated into the natural cycle. The process necessary for creating capital thus begins before the commodity, and ends after the exchange.[7] According to Jorn, only this complete cycle can provide us with a scientific view of the process of production and consumption in the capitalist economy.

By taking as his starting point the materialist concept of form and the resulting schema, Jorn analyses the transformation of the object of utility into a commodity. Three conditions are necessary for this to occur:

(a) that the usefulness of the object must be as universal as possible so as to be desired by a maximum number of consumers (hence, historically speaking, the transition from craft to industry),
(b) that objects be interchangeable (leading to mass production),
(c) that consumption rise to ever higher levels (for which purpose, advertising is used).

The transition from use to exchange – upon which question Marxist economists remain rather discreet – is of the greatest importance, in Jorn's view, to our understanding of the capitalist production cycle. This is because, for an object of utility to become an object of exchange, it must first be shorn of all *immediate* utility : its transformation into a commodity implies thus its devalorization. In actual use, the usefulness of the object lies in its quality as an object : it is therefore valorized as an object of utility through its utilization. Conversely, however, the slightest utilization devalorizes it as an object of mercantile exchange. The transition is the one that occurs from *quality* to *quantity*. The commodity therefore appears as a socialized object of utility, as a quality becomes quantity.

According to this view, money is apprehended, from the point of view of economics, as a totally socialized commodity; for it to serve as the yardstick of value for other commodities it first had to lose all value in-itself (and hence any possibility of being useful). It is not only a mass-produced commodity, it has no value outside the series of banknotes to which it belongs.[8]

The transition from object of utility to commodity, as presented by Jorn, also accounts for the phenomenon of the primitive accumulation of capital or the formation of social saving. Under the *ancien régime*, it was disaffection for objects of utility that enabled the merchant to hoard or store his goods. Storage is an early form of saving, and the accumulation of savings (i.e. non-consumption) made possible the formation of social capital and the vast increase in wealth. By denying the necessity of saving, Marx conceived of the economy as a closed system of production and consumption: yet, without accumulation of wealth, without *economizing*, there can be no science of economy. Any economic policy applying the Marxian reasoning results in an a-economic conception of the economy seen as a process of reproduction. It would be a 'biological economy', in which all production is fully consumed.[9]

Concrete utopia: the realization of art

Jorn views Marx first and foremost as a defender of the poor, pleading in his day the cause of the proletarian, who had no other property than his own person. His arguments are convincing to whoever is already convinced, but he was incapable of developing them into a vigorous case because of his confusion of science with technique. Lacking a precise concept of science, he saw no other way of coming to the rescue of the proletariat than through the abolition of surplus value. Carried out to the letter, his system effectively results in the suppression of saving.[10]

Marx correctly noted that capitalist accumulation presupposed saving, and that the suppression of saving implied the same for surplus value. Jorn, on the other hand, states that surplus value has always existed, the excess of production over reproduction constituting the wealth of all societies.

It is through surplus value that we create wealth: society's members may enjoy it *as consumers*. The socialization of consumption stems from the logic of the capitalist process itself, since the latter *socializes* objects of utility, i.e. makes them available for the consumption of each and everyone in the form of commodities.

Consequently, the aim of economic socialism (the suppression of surplus value) theoretically leads to a contraction of consumption, and to a growing 'privatization' of it. But at the same time, the *political* conception of the State (on the one hand, the State is viewed as an 'apparatus' to be made use of in order to apply a specific economic policy, while on the other hand it is denied and its suppression demanded)[11] derives from the same absurdity; the *partisan* concept of the State views it as a substance and not as a form – 'the perfect form', notes Jorn, as did Hegel – of higher organization of society. In this respect, the State is the locus where the conflicts and excesses of partisan politics cancel each other out.

Marxist socialism thereby managed to achieve the contrary to what Marx's economic project set out to achieve (the accession of the poorest class to ownership of the means of production): it reduced the number of owners to one single owner, the State. Economic equality was achieved through the impoverishment of all.

Jorn countered the pure concept of political revolution with one of his own: the artistic revolution. The former results in the devalorization of man (where quality turns into quantity) and to generalized reification. He, on the other hand, foresees the replacement of authoritarian socialism by its contrary: a value-liberating society. According to this dialectic, a world of creation will follow upon the world of economy. In this new world, Jorn concludes, the changing of the conditions of existence will be the works of the producers themselves, *become creators*.

Notes and references

Introduction

1 Karl Marx, *Capital*, Book 1, pt 8 (Moscow, Foreign Languages Publishing House, 1954), p. 763.
2 The bulk of the proletariat engaged came from the Faubourg St. Antoine, then outside Paris proper.
3 This phrase is typical: 'We consider the tendency of modern industry to associate children and young people of both sexes in the great movement of social production as a progress and a legitimate tendency, although the manner in which this tendency is manifested under the yoke of capital is an abomination. In a rational society, *any child over the age of nine* should be a productive worker.' K. Marx, *Résolutions du premier congrès de l'A.I.T.*, (1866), in J. Freymond (ed.), *La première internationale* (Geneva, 1962), vol. 1, p. 31, and K. Marx, F. Engels, *Werke* (Berlin, 1957), vol. 16, p. 193.
4 Which is not to say that Marxism had no liberating quality to it by comparison with that other power ideology, liberalism. Historically, however, it served to effect a revolution for power, and not for its destruction. Once it became operative, moreover, Marxism no longer existed in its pure state: it had become Kautskyism, Austro-Marxism, Guesdism, Leninism. . . . After 1917 we may speak of Marxism–Leninism as the most fully developed form of the bureaucratic class's ideology.
5 Which is not to say he had not consumed before this. But he had absorbed no more than a minimum of the Gross National Product, just enough for his physical reproduction; his global demand was therefore too negligible to encourage any noteworthy investment.
6 Thus, reversing Lenin's formula (in *What is to be Done?*), we may say that the consciousness of the proletariat is revolutionary the moment it ceases to come from the exterior.

1 The Soviet State: myths and realities (1917–21)

1 See Pierre Broué, a Trotskyist academic, who vigorously defends this viewpoint: preface to O. Anweiler, *Les soviets en Russie* (Paris, 1972). See my review of this book in *Esprit*, 5 (May 1973).

2 As attested by O. Anweiler, *Die Rätebewegung in Russland (1905–1921)* (Leiden, 1958), p. 24.

3 ibid., p. 45.

4 According to Anweiler, the first ones appeared in May 1905 at Ivanovo-Voznesensk. The anarchist Volin claims it was at the end of January at St Petersburg but gives no proof of this. See Volin (V. H. Eichenbaum), *La révolution inconnue* (Paris, 1947; repr. 1969), partly translated into English in 2 vols, *Nineteen-Seventeen* (London, 1954) and *The Unknown Revolution* (London, 1955; Detroit and Chicago, 1974).

5 In his memoirs the Ukrainian anarchist, Nestor Makhno, provides a lively description of the way the *skhod* assemblies transformed themselves into soviets by simply changing their names in 1917; the situation must have been rather similar in 1905, at least in rural areas. See *La révolution russe en Ukraine* (Paris, 1970), pt 1.

6 Anweiler, op. cit., p. 128.

7 ibid., pp. 130, 133.

8 Honest Leninists do not even deny this any longer. See the historian M. Liebman's *Le léninisme sous Lénine* (Paris, 1973), p. 155, which notes that on 27 February 1917 the Bolsheviks had still not overcome their misgivings of 1905.

9 Anweiler, op. cit., pp. 93–5.

10 ibid., p. 98.

11 ibid., p. 213.

12 Though not over the Pan-Russian Soviet of peasant delegates whose congress, which met in November 1918, rejected Lenin as President of the Council of People's Commissars.

13 Cf. the opinion of the Menshevik, Skobelev, Minister of Labour in the Provisional Government, for whom the management and control of industry was to be a State function, the working class's role being limited to one of assistance and support in relation to the public authorities. Cited by M. Brinton, *The Bolsheviks and Workers' Control* (1970), pp. 4–5; this pamphlet, conceived chronologically, is extremely useful in unravelling the skein of decrees and resolutions concerning workers' control.

14 *Fabzavkomy* = *Fabrichno-zavodnye komitety*.

15 Anweiler, op. cit., pp. 155–8.

16 A Soviet historian shares this view while expressing, with a certain objectivity in her presentation of the facts, the view of her Party: A. Pankratova, *Fabzavkomii Rossii v borbie za socialisticheskuiu fabriku* (Moscow, 1923). Long excerpts are available in French in *Autogestion*, 4 (December 1967).

17 Brinton, op. cit., p. 15.

18 Pankratova in *Autogestion*, p. 49.

19 P. Avrich, 'The Bolshevik Revolution and Workers' Control in Russian Industry', *Slavic Review*, xxii, 1 (March 1963).

20 Brinton, op. cit., p. 16.

21 Avrich, op. cit.; for further details see Avrich's thesis, *The Russian Revolution and the Factory Committees* (Ann Arbor, Mich., University Microfilms, 1973).

22 Pankratova, op. cit., speaks, deprecatingly, of 'autonomous production communes', and Brinton, op. cit., pp. 29, 30, reproduces accounts which corroborate this, given by trade union congress delegates.

23 Ideas he had already expressed in April and June 1917! Cited by Brinton, op. cit., pp. 3, 5.

24 Cf. e.g. the first all-Russian conference of factory committees (17–22 October 1917), where a resolution on these lines was approved as the result of a Bolshevik–Menshevik alliance.

25 My italics. See Pankratova, op. cit., at end.

26 Cf. A. Kollontai, *L'Opposition ouvrière* (Paris, repr. 1974). Despite Kollontai's lyrical style, it is worth recalling that in 1920 the trade unionists already constituted a solid bureaucracy within the State. Underneath the libertarian rhetoric of this pamphlet lies a struggle for power insofar as the trade union leader-

ship controlled the process of enrolment of communists in the union apparatus. This could eventually give them a majority in the Party. That is why the unions were made subject to Party 'centralism', to which moreover even the Party's extreme left wing was attached. The demise of union autonomy signalled the end of union bureaucracy's independence of the politicians and not that of the masses (which had already been lost three years previously). In the final analysis, all the left oppositionists finished by returning to the Leninist fold. See R. V. Daniels, *The Conscience of the Revolution* (Cambridge, Mass., 1960), pp. 121–5.

27 The sources for all documentation are still: Makhno's memoirs, 3 vols (1929, 1936, 1937), of which only vol. 1, has been translated from Russian (*La révolution russe en Ukraine*, Paris, repr. 1970). These memoirs unfortunately only take us up to 1918. We also have P. Arshinov's detailed account, *Istorija makhnovskogo dvizenija* (Berlin, 1923), translated into English under the title *History of the Makhnovist Movement (1918–1921)* (Detroit and Chicago, 1974). From the communist side we have M. Kubanin, *Mahnovščina* (Leningrad, n.d.). The other works are mainly drawn from the above documents. The following may be consulted: D. Footman, *Civil War in Russia* (London, 1961), which sets the Ukrainian episode in the context of the civil war (ch. 6, 'Makhno'). Volin, op. cit., uses Arshinov's account while adding his personal reminiscences.

28 Footman, op. cit., p. 269.

29 S. Singleton, 'The Tambov Revolt (1920–1921)', *Slavic Review*, xxv, 3 (September 1966).

30 V. Lenin, *The Development of Capitalism in Russia* (Moscow; 1st Russian edn dates from 1899).

31 See Daniels' praiseworthy attempt to conceptualize a left–right schema better suited to Bolshevik reality, op. cit., intro.; for Trotsky's position in the schema, see pp. 107–10, 121–5.

32 L. Trotsky, *Terrorisme et communisme* (Paris, 1963; 1st edn in Russia, July 1920), p. 254. Most of the passages

cited are taken from speeches made either at the Third Russian Congress of Trade Unions (April 1920) or that of the Soviets of the National Economy, or else at the Tenth Congress of the CPSU (March 1921).

33 ibid., pp. 221, 219, 217.

34 ibid., p. 217.

35 ibid., p. 215.

36 ibid., pp. 213–14.

37 ibid., pp. 203, 205.

38 ibid., p. 229.

39 Cited by Brinton, op. cit., p. 61.

40 Cited ibid., p. 61.

41 ibid., p. 67.

42 A good many accounts of the Petrograd strike are available. Cf. Alexander Berkman, *Die Kronstadt Rebellion* (Berlin, 1923), pp. 3–5; Victor Serge, *Memoirs of a Revolutionary* (London, 1967); and Ida Mett, *La Commune de Kronstadt* (Paris, 1949), pp. 27–30.

43 See P. Avrich, *Kronstadt 1921* (Princeton, 1970), still the most complete work on the subject, given currently available documentation.

44 ibid., p. 190.

45 No. 7 (8 March 1921). The slogan 'All power to the soviets and not to the parties' recurs frequently in several editions of *Izvestia*.

46 For the conflict between authoritarians and anti-authoritarians in the First International see F. Brupbacher, *Marx und Bakunin* (Munich, 1922; repr. Berlin, 1969).

47 *The Russian Revolution and the Communist Party* (Berlin, 1922). This is a pamphlet written in June 1921 by four well-known Russian anarchists and sent to Rudolf Rocker in Germany, who made a first translation which I have not been able to find. This one is due to A. Berkman, who had just arrived in Berlin at the time.

48 P. C. Masini, 'Gli anarchici italiani e la rivoluzione russa', *Rivista storica del socialismo* (1962).

49 ibid. Malatesta developed this idea and went on to speak of a 'new governing class' in his preface to L. Fabbri, *Dittatura e rivoluzione* (Rome, 1921).

50 Cf. E. Goldman, *My Disillusionment in Russia* (New York, 1923), preface.

51 A. Berkman, *The Anti-Climax* (Berlin, 1925). Berkman and Emma

Goldman spent the years 1920 and 1921 in Russia, to which they had been deported by the American authorities. Their pro-Bolshevik fervour dwindled rapidly, but it took two painful years before they dared break with the Bolshevik government that had welcomed them as distinguished guests.

52 ibid. The social-revolutionary account comes from D. Gavronski, *Le bilan du bolchévisme russe* (Paris, 1920; written January 1919), p. 42. Cf. also P. Avrich, *The Russian Anarchists* (Princeton, 1967), ch. 5.

53 A. Souchy, *Wie lebt der Arbeiter und der Bauer in Russland und in der Ukraine* (Berlin, n.d.), preface. Souchy belonged to the leadership of the German anarcho-syndicalist federation (FAUD) and visited Russia between April and October 1920. His account is sober and objective; the preface dates from December 1920.

54 E. Goldman, *The Crushing of the Russian Revolution* (London, n.d.). See also the pamphlet by Rudolf Rocker, the German theoretician of anarcho-syndicalism, *Der Bankrott des russischen Staatskommunismus* (n.p., 1921), pp. 100–1.

55 J. Sadoul, *Notes sur la révolution bolchévique* (Paris, 1919), pp. 286–7. The figures cited are those given by Avrich, *The Russian Anarchists*, p. 173, n.7.

56 Mauricius, *Au pays des soviets* (Paris, n.d. [1921]), pp. 153–4. The Russian anarcho-syndicalist position is set forth in G. P. Maksimov, *Syndicalists in the Russian Revolution* (London, n.d.).

57 Goldman, *My Disillusionment in Russia*; G. Leval, 'Choses de Russie', *Le Libertaire* (11–18 November 1921); and Souchy, op. cit., preface. Gaston Leval had gone to Russia in order to take part in the congress of the Red International of Trade Unions in 1921, held in Moscow. He played a role in obtaining the release of imprisoned Russian anarchists, the latter then being deported directly abroad.

58 Apart from the anarchists cited above, see the account by the Spanish delegate to the second congress of the Third International (July–August 1920): A. Pestaña, *Informe*

de mi estancia en la URSS (Madrid, repr. 1968).

59 Souchy, op. cit., describes with great precision the process whereby the unions became nationalized organs of production (*verstaatlicht*) and how the administrative delegates in the villages behaved like *ancien régime* landowners.

60 The terms 'State capitalism' and 'new class' recur frequently in anarchist writings. Cf. e.g.: *The Russian Revolution and the Communist Party*, op. cit., p. 24; Volin, *Le fascisme rouge* (Brussels, n.d.), and *Bolševickaia diktatura v svece anarxisma* (Paris, 1928), pp. 26, 27; Rocker, op. cit., p. 58, speaks of a 'commissarocracy'; Souchy, op. cit., pp. 66, 89; Luigi Fabbri and Errico Malatesta speak of a 'new class' (from 1919 on, cf. Masini, op. cit.); and Arthur [Müller] Lehning uses the term 'bureaucratic State' (*Anarchismus und Marxismus in der russischen Revolution*, Fr. trans. Paris, 1971, a text which first appeared in *Die Internationale*). For a summary, see Avrich, *The Russian Anarchists*, pp. 191–4, and his 'On the New Class: a Libertarian Critique', *Libertarian Analysis* (New York), vol. 1, no. 1 (winter 1970). The *Encyclopédie anarchiste* (ed. S. Faure, 1924) defined *Bolshevism* as a State capitalism founded on the enforced subjugation and exploitation of the masses. Cf. also *La revue anarchiste* (Paris), which speaks in terms of a 'dominating caste' and mentions the Makhnovshchina (no. 4, April 1922; no. 17, May–June 1923; no. 21, November 1923).

61 These theses were developed by Trotsky in *The Revolution Betrayed* (New York, 1945), notably in the chapter 'What is the USSR?'. In addition we may cite his last utterance on this subject ('following the Second World War either there will be a world revolution or the USSR will relapse to the stage of capitalism') in *Defense of Marxism* (New York, 1939).

62 M. Yvon, *Ce qu'est devenu la révolution russe* (n.p., n.d. [1936]), pp. 85–6. See in particular the 3rd *causerie*, 'L'Etat et les classes'.

63 See, e.g., in France, the organ of the Union communiste (a tiny dissident Trotskyist group): *L'Internationale*,

no. 21 (23 May 1936), 'La nouvelle constitution soviétique'.

64 The tribulations of the American Trotskyists (Schachtman, Burnham) also led them into conflict with Trotsky over the question of the workers' State; but apart from Raya Dunayevskaya's *Marxism and Freedom*, which was only published in 1958, the level of discussion was less theoretical than in France and, above all, led to a total break with the revolutionary movement. Thus Burnham's managerial class had nothing to do with any class reality but more with a *stratum*. Far from superseding Trotsky's analysis he actually returns to it, though in a conservative perspective (see *The Managerial Revolution*, New York, 1941). Rizzi's book was published in Paris at his own expense with a print order of 500 copies: B. R[izzi], *La bureaucratisation du monde* (n.d. [1939]).

65 For further details about Socialisme ou Barbarie, see 'Socialisme ou Barbarie', *Socialisme ou Barbarie* (Paris), no. 1 (March 1949); P. Chaulieu,

'Les rapports de production en Russie', ibid., no. 2 (May–June 1949); P. Chaulieu, 'L'exploitation des paysans sous le capitalisme bureaucratique', ibid., no. 4 (October–November 1949). See also by Castoriadis (= Chaulieu), 'Sur la dégénérescence de la révolution russe', and 'Conception et programme de Socialisme ou Barbarie', in *La société bureaucratique* (Paris, 1973), vol. 2, pp. 373–92 and 392–416. In English see P. Cardan, *From Bolshevism to the Bureaucracy* (London, n.d.), and *Modern Capitalism and Revolution* (n.p., n.d.). See also his *Socialism or Barbarism*. These three (Solidarity) pamphlets resume and adapt rather than translate Chaulieu's central points. For greater detail about the ideology of Socialisme ou Barbarie, see A. Gombin, *The Origins of Modern Leftism* (Penguin Books, 1975), ch. 1.

66 On Trotskyism's attitude towards the USSR, see C. Lefort, 'Les contradictions de Trotsky et le problème révolutionnaire', *Les temps modernes*, 39 (January 1949).

2   The radical tradition in Russia

1 For the evolution of social thought in Russia before 1850 we have A. Herzen's well-informed and highly lucid account, *Du développement des idées en Russie* (London, 1853, published in French). See also P. Pascal's rather more philosophically committed *Les grands courants de la pensée russe contemporaine* (Lausanne, 1971).

2 Thus Bakunin, in an article in *Deutsche Jahrbücher* (1842), under the pseudonym Jules Elysard.

3 M. Malia, *Alexander Herzen and the Birth of Russian Socialism* (Cambridge, Mass., 1961), p. 99.

4 G. Sourine, *Le fouriérisme en Russie* (Paris, 1936), *passim*.

5 R. Labry, *Alexandre Ivanovič Herzen* (Paris, 1928), ch. 1.

6 ibid.

7 Sourine, op. cit., pp. 58–9.

8 Cf. Isaiah Berlin's introduction to A. Herzen, *My Past and Thoughts*, 4 vols (London, 1968).

9 R. Labry, *Herzen et Proudhon* (Paris, 1928), p. 39.

10 It is worth adding that a distinct social differentiation grew up among the Cossacks under the shelter of this autonomy: the masters on the one hand; farmers, fishermen and soldiers on the other.

11 Cf. P. Pascal, *Le révolte de Pougatchev* (Paris, 1971).

12 Because he enunciated the ideas of his age rather than enclose them within a grand design, Herzen left no single work containing the quintessence of his thought. His socialism emerges gradually in his writings. In French, *Le monde russe et la révolution (Mémoires d'A. Herzen)* (Paris, 1860–2); *Lettres de France et d'Italie* (Geneva, 1871). In English, *My Past and Thoughts*, op. cit.; *From the Other Shore* (London, 1856), are among those to be consulted. The most complete Russian edition after M. K. Lemke's, *Polnoe sobrane socinenij i pisem*, 22 vols (Petrograd, 1915–25), is now the *Sobranie socinenij v tridcati tomah*, 34 vols (Moscow, 1954–66).

13 Herzen himself was to experience the full rigour of this arbitrariness, subjected to imprisonment, deportation and exile. Cf. E. H. Carr, *The Romantic Exiles* (London, 1949; 1st edn 1933). Carr rather tends to exaggerate the romanticism in Herzen's thought and certainly overdoes his 'lordly' suffering.
14 E. Lampert, *Studies in Rebellion* (London, 1957), p. 238.
15 Malia, op. cit., p. 410.
16 Herzen, *From the Other Shore*, p. 240.
17 Berlin's introduction to *My Past and Thoughts*.
18 In the *IXe Lettre de France et d'Italie* (1849).
19 *From the Other Shore*.
20 *The Bell* (Geneva), no. 2, repr. in Lemke, op. cit., vol. 20, pp. 131–5.
21 Lampert, op. cit., pp. 196ff.
22 Malia, op. cit., p. 132.
23 Cited by Lampert, op. cit., p. 233.
24 'Letters to an Old Comrade', cited by R. Labry, *Alexander Ivanovič Herzen*, op. cit., p. 395.
25 It could acquire status by registration with the guild of merchants, whose upper strata really did constitute an industrial and merchant bourgeoisie; but in 1845 this category included no more than 1,800 persons. This class only began to take on some numerical importance with the industrial revolution at the end of the century. See R. Portal, *Les slaves* (Paris, 1965), p. 186.
26 There is no paradox in the fact that the most radical theorists today have resuscitated the aristocratic mentality in its most ludic and most disinterested form. See R. Vaneigem, *Traité de savoir vivre à l'usage des jeunes générations*, Paris 1967, p. 81.
27 F. Venturi, *Roots of Revolution: a History of the Populist and Socialist Movements in Nineteenth Century Russia* (New York, 1966), p. 138ff. The first edition was published in 1952 under the title, *Il populismo russo*. The American edition is slightly more complete.
28 ibid., p. 297.
29 Cf. A. Coquart, *Dmitri Pisarev (1840–1868) et l'idéologie du nihilisme russe* (Paris, 1946).
30 *Narodnaia rasprava*, no. 2, cited by Venturi, op. cit., p. 383–4.
31 Venturi, op. cit., ch. 16.

32 By an ironic twist of fate, it was Ogarev who had given the signal for the 'Go to the People' movement in an article published in *Kolokol* (the Bell), in 1861. Both he and Herzen believed that the peasantry was the repository of revolutionary dynamism, and that inspiration should be drawn from that class.
33 Venturi, op. cit., ch. 21.
34 A. Gerschenkron, 'The Problem of Economic Development in Russian Intellectual History of the Nineteenth Century', in E. J. Simmons (ed.), *Continuity and Change in Russian and Soviet Thought* (Cambridge, Mass., 1955).
35 Portal, op. cit., p. 282.
36 Venturi, op. cit., p. 539.
37 G. Fischer, *Russian Liberalism* (Cambridge, Mass., 1958), pp. 49, 61. It is interesting to note that there were numerous contacts between liberals and Marxists to begin with. They originated from the same class and they shared a common objective (power), but they differed over the question of means : the liberals were to opt for reformism, applying a strategy which devolved upon the social democrats in Germany.
38 Of the 425 revolutionary agitators arrested in 1877–8 and considered as 'criminal', 147 were nobles, 90 were clergymen, 58 sons of officers, 54 came from the *mieshchanstvo*, 11 were soldiers and 65 of peasant origin. See Venturi, op. cit., p. 595.
39 ibid., p. 383–4.
40 M. Bakunin, transl. from *Etatisme et anarchie* (Leiden, 1967; 1st edn 1873), p. 234.
41 Article in *L'Egalite* (27 July 1869), and repr. in M. Bakounine, *Oeuvres* (Paris, 1895–1911), vol. 5, p. 129. See also Article 8 of the Programme of the Slav Section of Zurich, repr. as appendix to *Etatisme et anarchie*.
42 *Oeuvres*, vol. 4, p. 476–7.
43 *Etatisme et anarchie*, p. 319.
44 *Narodnoe delo* (September 1868), cited by Venturi, op. cit., p. 432.
45 P. Avrich, *The Russian Anarchists* (Princeton, N.J., 1967), pp. 19, 92.
46 The Russified form of his name is Makhaev; his doctrine is designated by the term *makhaevshchina*, along with the movement it inspired. The first two sections of this work were written in Siberia in 1898 and 1899,

the third being written in Geneva. The work as a whole was printed in Geneva under the title *Umstvennyj rabočij* (The Mental Worker) in 1904–6 and signed with the pseudonym A. Volskij. The first two sections were also published in St Petersburg in 1906. A new edition was published in the USA (New York–Baltimore) in 1968 by Inter-Language Literary Associates. The first section, the most interesting, is entitled 'The Evolution of Social Democracy'; the second, 'Scientific Socialism'; the third (I) 'Socialism and the Workers' Movement in Russia' and (II) 'Socialist Science as a New Religion'. Machajski also published pamphlets and two reviews. Most of his papers are deposited in the International Institute for Social History in Amsterdam. His thought has been popularized in the West by Max Nomad: cf. *Aspects of Revolt* (New York, 1961), esp. ch. 5.

47 In an unpublished manuscript entitled 'The Bankruptcy of Socialism in the Nineteenth Century', Machajski points out that he is speaking of the professional intelligentsia, paid on a salaried basis, as opposed to those living off rents or profits.

48 In his preface to 'The Mental Worker' Machajski even draws a parallel between Christ and Marx, stating that both of them expressed the people's yearning for liberation (p. 43 of the 1968 American edn).

49 *Bilans buržuazyjnej rewolucyj rosyjskiej* (Geneva, 1909: Max Nomad Foundation at IISH, Amsterdam).

50 *Burźuaznaja revolucija i rabočoe delo* (n.p., 1905: Max Nomad Foundation at IISH, Amsterdam).

51 'Rabočij Zagovor'.

52 Max Nomad attributes dictatorial ambitions to Machajski within the proposed conspiracy (*Aspects of Revolt*, end of ch. 5). There is nothing, however, to corroborate Nomad's suspicions, which he only made public after thirty years' silence! Against this view see M. S. Shatz, *Anti-intellectualism in the Russian Intelligentsia* (mimeo., New York, 1963: Certificate of Russian Institute, Colombia University), p. 75.

53 Cf. A. d'Agostino, 'Intelligentsia Socialism and the "Workers'

Revolution": the Views of J. W. Machajski', *International Review of Social History*, vol. 1, xiv (1969), pp. 74–5.

54 *Burźuaznaja revolucija i rabočoe delo*, op. cit., and M. S. Shatz, 'The Makhaevists and the Russian Revolutionary Movement', *International Review of Social History*, vol. 2, xv (1970).

55 *Rabočaja revolucija*, no. 1 (single issue) (Moscow, June–July 1918). Machajski wrote every page of this journal himself in May 1918.

56 Novomirski, *Čto takoe anarhizm* (n.p. [Geneva], 1907), ch. ix. Among Machajskist writings (those more or less faithful to his ideas) we should mention: E. I. Lozinskij, *Čto že takoe, nakonec, intelligencija?* (What, in the Final Analysis, is the Intelligentsia?) (St Petersburg, 1907); and K. Orgeiani (G. Gogelija), *Ob intelligencii* ('On the Intelligentsia') (London, 1912).

57 Avrich, op. cit., p. 19.

58 It was the 1917 Revolution and the resulting persecution which led the anarchists to develop their analysis of Bolshevism or, rather, of the Soviet State, as we have seen in ch. 1.

59 J. H. L. Keep, *The Rise of Social Democracy in Russia* (Oxford, 1963), p. 39. There was very little differentiation between 'economists' and social democrats before the beginning of the twentieth century. The publication of *Credo* by Prokopovitch and Kuskova was to put an end to this state of affairs. It is worth noting that it was the 'legal Marxist', Struve, who drew up the party programme for the First Congress of the RSDWP (1898).

60 Who did not hesitate to predict that 'though today they[Leninists] might man the barricades, tomorrow they might well occupy the judges' seats'. Cited by Keep, op. cit., p. 61.

61 P. Axelrod, 'Ob"edinienie rossijskoj socialdemokratij i eja zadači' ('The Unification of Russian Social Democracy and its Tasks) in *Iskra*, nos 55, 57 (15 December 1903, 15 January 1904).

62 ibid., Axelrod refers to the passage in the *18th Brumaire of Louis Bonaparte* in which Marx writes: 'Its gladiators (the spokesmen of bourgeoisie)

found the ideals and the forms, the means of self-deception, they needed, that they might hide from themselves the bourgeois limitations of the struggle in which they were engaged. . . .' (London, 1926, p. 25).

63 L. Trotsky, *Nos tâches politiques* (Paris, 1971), p. 20. Significantly, Trotsky never authorized the reprinting of this pamphlet in his lifetime. Although it was first published in Geneva in 1904 (in Russian), a revealing pointer to the ideological development of the extreme left lies in the fact that the French translation was only published in the wake of the events of May 1968.

64 ibid., p. 189.

65 L. Trotsky, *Rapport de la délégation sibérienne* (Paris, 1970), *passim*.

66 *Nos tâches politiques*, p. 35.

67 ibid., p. 144, n. 7. Those who have followed Trotsky's career as a member of the Council of People's Commissars will surely savour this text, written in 1904. It was not the last time Trotsky elaborated a critique whose bitter irony would be later illustrated by history.

68 D. Guérin, *Rosa Luxemburg et la spon-* *tanéité révolutionnaire* (Paris, 1971), pp. 42–4.

69 Cited by Guérin, ibid.

70 V. Lenin, *Un pas en avant, deux pas en arrière* (Moscow), p. 210. In this passage, the author replies to the criticisms of Axelrod contained in the *Iskra* article mentioned. Italics are those of the original text.

71 Article by R. Luxemburg in *Neue Zeit* (1904). An English translation is available under the title 'Leninism or Marxism' in R. Luxemburg, *The Russian Revolution* (Ann Arbor, Mich., 1961).

72 ibid., and R. Luxemburg, *La révolution russe*, in *Oeuvres*, vol. 2 (Paris, 1969), p. 85 (the latter text was written in September–October 1918).

73 She was active in the Polish (SDKPiL) and the German parties, but she also maintained close links with the Russian party – of which the Polish party was an integral part from 1906 to 1912.

74 G. Fischer in *Russian Liberalism*, op. cit., rightly insists on what the liberals and the social democrats had in common: both held an evolutionary view of history completely lacking in the liberal bourgeoisie in the West (cf. ch. 3, 'Third Force').

3 Council communism

1 As we have seen in ch. 1.

2 Generally, we find three tendencies: the moderate, chauvinist branch; the reformist, pacifist branch, less inclined to seek integration into bourgeois democracy; the revolutionary left wing, the majority of which ended by siding with the Third International.

3 Here I am employing Gustav Landauer's distinction (in *Die Revolution*, Frankfurt, 1907) between *topia*, which is experienced and expressed reality, and *utopia*, incorporating both topia – that which exists – and that which is not expressed, but to which we aspire. The moment utopia becomes a fact it becomes topia.

4 F. L. Carsten, *Revolution in Central Europe (1918–1919)* (London, 1972), p. 125ff.

5 For a chronological and institutional description see A. Schwarz, *Die* *Weimarer Republik* (Corstanz, 1958), p. 28–9.

6 P. Broué, *Révolution en Allemagne* (Paris, 1971), ch. 6.

7 P. von Oertzen, *Betriebsräte in Novemberrevolution* (Düsseldorf, 1963), p. 71ff.

8 Broué, op. cit., and E. Kolb, *Die Arbeiterräte in der deutschen Innenpolitik* (Düsseldorf, 1962), p. 60.

9 Kolb, op. cit., pp. 88–90.

10 ibid., pp. 91, 92.

11 This is the view of most historians of the period, starting with O. K. Flechtheim, even though the latter is favourable to the revolutionary movement. Cf. his *Die K.P.D. in der Weimarer Republik* (Frankfurt, 1969), ch. 2.

12 See R. Grunberger, *Red Rising in Bavaria* (London, 1973), for a chronology and account of these events. Documents of the period are to be found in G. Schmolze (ed.),

Revolution und Räterepublik in München 1918–1919 in Augenzeugenberichten (Düsseldorf, 1969).

13 The first council dates back to December 1917; cf. R. L. Tokés, *Béla Kun and the Hungarian Soviet Republic* (New York, 1967), p. 38. The vast literature on this subject is dealt with in F. Völgyes, *The Hungarian Soviet Republic* (Stanford, 1970).

14 Tokés, op. cit., p. 120.

15 ibid., p. 161.

16 Of the 33 People's Commissars, 17 were socialists, 14 communists and two belonged to no party (ibid., p. 137).

17 It is noteworthy that the Guilds, which were active after 1910, did not call for the ownership of industry, nor were they prepared to leave the management of industry in the hands of the workers alone. Finally, their theoreticians were careful to point out that there was no question of breaking with the unions and that they sought merely to transform the doctrines of trade-unionism, notably insofar as joint control was concerned. See G. D. H. Cole, *Guild Socialism* (London, 1920) p. 24.

18 G. D. H. Cole and R. Postgate, *The Common People* (London, 1968), p. 518.

19 ibid., p. 546–57.

20 Cf. B. Pribicevic, *The Shop Stewards' Movement and Workers' Control, 1910–1922* (Oxford, 1959), p. 99ff.

21 ibid., p. 144.

22 A. Tasca, *Naissance du fascisme* (Paris, 1967), p. 45.

23 ibid., p. 54.

24 ibid., p. 103–4.

25 H. Prouteau, *Les occupations d'usines en France et en Italie (1920–1936)* (Paris, 1967), p. 40.

26 J. M. Cammett, *Antonio Gramsci and the Origins of Italian Communism* (Stanford, 1967), p. 74.

27 'Sindicati e consigli', *Ordine Nuovo* (11 October 1919), in A. Gramsci, *L'Ordine Nuovo 1919–1920* (n.p., 1955), pp. 34–9 (henceforth referred to as *Opere*).

28 'Il partito e la revoluzione', *Ordine Nuovo* (27 December 1919), in *Opere*, pp. 67–71.

29 'Sindicalismo e consigli' *Ordine Nuovo* (8 November 1919), and second article, 'Sindicati e consigli' (20 June 1920), in *Opere*, pp. 44–8, 131–5.

30 'Democrazia operaia', *Ordine Nuovo* (21 July 1919), written in collaboration with Palmiro Togliatti, in *Opere*, pp. 10–13. See also J. M. Piotte, *La pensée politique de Gramsci* (Paris, 1970), p. 260.

31 Cammett, op. cit., p. 88.

32 Cf. 'Il problema del pottere', *Ordine Nuovo* (29 November 1919), and 'Partito di governo e classe di governo' (6 March 1920) in *Opere*, pp. 56–60, 91–6.

33 'Sindicati e consigli', op. cit. (20 June 1920).

34 Along similar lines, see Piotte, op. cit., p. 263.

35 Even though he openly held libertarian doctrines to be 'pernicious' (Cammett, op. cit., p. 125). Concerning his relations with the anarchists, cf. P. C. Masini, *Antonio Gramsci e l'Ordine Nuovo. Visti da un libertario* (n.p., 1956).

36 Cited by Piotte, op. cit., p. 271.

37 ibid., p. 373.

38 *Sozialistengesetze* (1878–90), which outlawed socialist organizations during this period. On the development of German social democracy see C. E. Schorske's classic work, *German Social Democracy (1905–1917)* (Cambridge, Mass. 1955).

39 R. Luxemburg, *The Mass Strike, the Political Party and the Trade Union* (Detroit, n. d. [1919]).

40 From the name of the journal opposing the leadership of the Dutch party, published from 1907 onwards: *Die Tribune*.

41 At the time she wrote, the problem of bureaucratization was being discussed widely. It was in 1906 (while still a member of the SPD) that Robert Michels drew attention to this phenomenon, before devoting a more detailed sociological study to it in 1911.

42 J. P. Nettl's book bears abundant witness to this: *Rosa Luxemburg* (London, 1966).

43 H. M. Bock, 'Zur Geschichte und Theorie der holländischen marxistischen Schule', in A. Pannekoek and H. Gorter, *Organisation und Taktik der proletarischen Revolution* (Frankfurt, 1969), p. 12, speaks of 500 members; F. Kool (ed.), in his introduction to *Die Linke gegen die Parteiherrschaft*

(Olten, 1970), p. 89, puts the figure at 700.

44 A. Pannekoek, *Die taktischen Differenzen in der Arbeiterbewegung* (Hamburg, 1909).

45 A. Pannekoek, 'Massenaktion und Revolution', *Die Neue Zeit*, vol. 1 (1912), p. 543, and 'Die Eroberung der Herrschaft', *Leipziger Volkszeitung*, no. 210 (1912).

46 A. Pannekoek, 'Marxistische Theorie und revolutionäre Taktik', *Die Neue Zeit*, vol. 1 (1912), pp. 272–81, 365–73. On the history of 'left-wing radicalism', cf. H. M. Bock, *Syndikalismus und Linkskommunismus von 1918–1923* (Meisenheim am Glan, 1969).

47 The more so in that extreme-left journals circulated with amazing ease, even at the front. Cf. J. Miller, 'Zur Geschichte der linken Sozial-demokraten in Bremen (1906–1918)', in *Zeitschrift für Geschichtswissenschaft* (Sonderheft, 1958), pp. 202–17.

48 In reality, a good many Spartakists did not share the views of their leaders but, in the circumstances, only the latter managed to make their views heard. Liebknecht's views, moreover, were more innovative than those of Luxemburg, as is shown by his prison writings in the years 1917–18: Karl Liebknecht, *Politische Aufzeichnungen aus seinem Nachlass* (Berlin, 1921). See also Bock, op. cit., pp. 65, 66.

49 *Arbeiterpolitik* (Bremen), no. 1 (24 January 1916), and no. 7 (17 February 1917), see the editorials.

50 To begin with, the ISD label, strictly speaking, referred only to the Hamburg and Bremen groups. But within a short space of time all the extremist groups came to be known by this name.

51 *Arbeiterpolitik* (Bremen), no. 15 (14 April 1917), and no. 10 (26 August 1916).

52 'Zur Einführung', *Vorbote* (1 January 1916), unsigned.

53 A. Pannekoek, 'Bolschewismus und Demokratie', *Arbeiterpolitik* (Bremen), no. 5 (14 December 1918).

54 Radek played a vital role in this unexpected rapprochement. Having been active in the Hamburg organization, he joined Lenin in 1917 and argued in favour of reunification. It should be added that the Bolshevik leaders were highly popular among the Internationals, the latter reprinting articles by Lenin, Zinoviev and, of course, Radek in their press, even though the latter had not exactly left fond memories behind him among his former comrades in either the German or Polish parties.

55 More exactly, the divergencies were masked by a façade of ideological unity. Thus, even at the constitutive conference of the USPD (in April 1917), the Spartakist representative, Fritz Rück, had expressed views very close to those of the Internationals. H. M. Bock, *Syndikalismus und Linkskommunismus*, op. cit., p. 62.

56 *Programm der kommunistischen Arbeiter-Partei Deutschlands*, place of publication not indicated, undated [1920].

57 It was the left-wing communists of Hamburg and Bremen who drew up the statutes of the AAUD in August 1919. Cf. Bock, op. cit., pp. 130–2. See also F. Wolffheim, *Betriebsorganisationen oder Gewerkschaften* (Hamburg, 1919; the text dates from August).

58 *Massenaktion*, pamphlet put out by the KAU (Berlin, 1933). For a long time already, the AAUD–E had been torn between those wanting to maintain a solid organization, with decisions taken at the top and binding on the rank-and-file (the *Rätekommunisten*), and those calling for the abolition of all constricting organizational structures. As for propaganda, chiefly directed against the political parties, it called for the extension of the councils' watchword. Cf. *Die Allgemeine Arbeiter-Union (Einheitsorganisation). Was sie ist und was sie will!* (Frankfurt am Main, 1927).

59 H. M. Bock, op. cit., p. 209. In 1923, council communist groups and sects as a whole numbered fewer than 20,000 persons (F. Kool, op. cit., p. 145).

60 Rosa Luxemburg had expressed reservations concerning three points: the principle of nationalities, the non-collectivization of land, the dictatorship of the party. These reservations came on top of her

reluctance to break with social democracy, at least up to December 1918. Cf. her *The Russian Revolution* (London, 1959; written in 1918).

61 A. Pannekoek, 'Bolschewismus und Demokratie', op. cit. See also his article, 'Der Anfang', *Arbeiterpolitik*, no. 48 (30 November 1918).

62 V. Lenin, *State and Revolution* (Moscow, 1970).

63 ibid. (italics in the original text).

64 O. C. Flechtheim, *Le parti communiste allemand sous la République de Weimar* (Paris, 1972), pp. 85ff. According to Broué, Paul Levi's effective authority over the party dates back to March 1919: op. cit., p. 295.

65 Letter in *Kommunistische Arbeiter-Zeitung* (Hamburg), no. 191 (1919).

66 V. Lenin, 'Left-Wing' Communism, an Infantile Disorder (Peking).

67 'Bericht über Moskau', *Die Aktion*, no. 39/40 (1920).

68 In *Manifestes, thèses et résolutions des quatre premiers congrès mondiaux de l'Internationale communiste* (Paris, 1934; facsimile repr. Paris, 1970), pp. 47, 49.

69 Bock, op. cit., p. 257.

70 Trotsky had no hesitation in criticizing in advance (at the Third Congress of the Communist International) this Fourth International 'in no danger of ever becoming very numerous'. He evidently thought otherwise when he set up his own Fourth International a few years later.

71 H. Gorter, *Offener Brief an den Genossen Lenin, eine Antwort auf Lenins Broschüre: Der Radikalismus, eine Kinderkrankheit des Kommunismus* (Berlin, n.d. [1921]).

72 F. Wolffheim, *Betriebsorganisationen oder Gewerkschaften* (Hamburg, 1919), and A. Pannekoek, *Weltrevolution und kommunistische Taktik* (Vienna, 1920).

73 'Der Parlamentarismus in der proletarischen Revolution', *Proletarier* (Berlin), no. 2 (November 1920).

74 'Zur Frage der Einheitschule', *Arbeiterpolitik* (Bremen), no. 7 (17 February 1917). Cf. also Bock, 'Zur Geschichte und Theorie der holländschen marxistischen Schule', op. cit., p. 17.

75 They were undoubtedly influenced by the founder of Dutch social democracy, who subsequently became a libertarian socialist, Ferdinand Domela Niewenhuis. From the 1890s on, Niewenhuis opposed parliamentarianism in favour of class struggle, and issued warnings to the Marxist parties, whom he suspected of veering towards State socialism and dictatorship. See his *Socialisme en danger*, 3rd edn (Paris, 1897), pp. 48, 72, 216.

76 O. Rühle, *Von der bürgerlichen zur proletarischen Revolution* (Berlin, 1970), p. 32 (the text dates from 1924).

77 ibid., pp. 38–43, and A. Pannekoek, *Workers' Councils* (Melbourne, 1950: English version of *De arbeidersraaden*, published in Amsterdam, 1946, under the pseudonym of P. Aartsz), p. 65. See also his 'Five Theses on the Class Struggle', *Southern Advocate for Workers' Councils* (Melbourne, May 1947).

78 J. H. [A. Pannekoek], 'Trade Unionism', *International Council Correspondence* (Chicago), no. 2 (January 1936).

79 H. Gorter, 'Partei, Klasse und Masse', *Proletarier*, no 4 (February–March 1921), and A. Pannekoek, 'Der neue Blanquismus', *Der Kommunist* (Bremen), no. 27 (1920).

80 [A. Pannekoek], 'Partei und Arbeiterklasse', *Rätekorrespondenz* (published by the GIC, the Dutch International Communist Group), no. 15 (March 1936), and J. Harper [A. Pannekoek], 'General Remarks on the Question of Organization', *Living Marxism* (Chicago), no. 5 (November 1938).

81 'Arbeiterräte und kommunistische Wirtschaftsgestaltung', *Rätekorrespondenz*, no 5 (October 1934).

82 A. Pannekoek, *Workers' Councils*, op. cit., section 1 : 'The Task'.

83 J. H. [A. Pannekoek], 'The Workers' Councils', *International Council Correspondence*, no. 5 (1936).

84 K. Horner [A. Pannekoek], *Sozialdemokratie und Kommunismus* (Hamburg, 1919).

85 K. Schröder, *Vom Werden der neuen Gesellschaft* (Berlin, n.d. [1920]); O. Rühle, *Von der bürgerlichen zur proletarischen Revolution*, op. cit.; J. Harper [A. Pannekoek], 'General Remarks on the Question of Organ-

ization', op. cit. See also the first programme of the KAPD (1920).

86 In general, it was the fervent KAPists who saw, in the existing factory organizations, the core of the councils. For a 'Council State', cf. the second programme of the KAPD (repr. in Bock, op. cit) and Pannekoek, who compares them to parliament (*Workers' Councils*, p. 47).

87 A detailed bio-bibliography of Gorter will be found in S. Bricianer, op. cit., and in Kool (èd.), *Die Linke gegen die Parteiherrschaft*, op. cit.

88 H. Gorter, 'Partei, Klasse und Masse', op. cit., and *Die Klassenkampf-Organisation des Proletariats* (Berlin, 1921). See also his *Offener Brief an den Genossen Lenin . . .*, op. cit.

89 Which he was to leave in order to return to the SPD in 1926. Concerning his life and work, cf. Kool's introduction to Kool, op. cit., and *Otto Rühle Schriften* (Hamburg, 1971).

90 O. Rühle, *Die Revolution ist keine Parteisache!* (Berlin, 1920), and *Von der bürgerlichen zur proletarischen Revolution*, op. cit.

91 A. Pannekoek: 'Historical Materialism', article published in Dutch in *Nieuwe Tijd*, 1919 (French translation in *Cahiers du communisme de conseils*, no. 1, 1968), and 'Marxismus und Idealismus', *Proletarier*, no. 4 (February–March 1921). A good biography of Pannekoek is to be found in *Die Linke gegen die Parteiherrschaft*. Bock gives a list of his books, articles and pamphlets in *Organisation und Taktik der proletarischen Revolution*, op. cit.

92 'Prinzip und Taktik', *Proletarier*, no. 8 (August 1927); 'Partei und Arbeiterklasse', *Rätekorrespondenz*, no. 15 (March 1936).

93 *Workers' Councils*, op. cit., p. 101, and 'The Party and the Working Class', *International Council Correspondence*, nos. 9 and 10 (September 1936). Cf. also Pannekoek's letter to Pierre Chaulieu, in which he further detailed his conception of the party-group, reprinted in *Cahiers du communisme de conseils*, no. 8 (May 1971).

94 See his *Revolutionshoffnungen* (Berlin, 1917), and Bock, op. cit., pp. 73ff. The Bremen ISD broke with

him, accusing him of having 'liquidated' the party-form.

95 ibid., p. 220.

96 H. Canne Meijer, 'Das Werden einer neuen Arbeiterbewegung', *Rätekorrespondenz*, nos 8–9 (April 1935), partial English translation in *International Council Correspondence*, no. 11 (August 1935). See also *Die Linke gegen die Parteiherrschaft*, op. cit., p. 613, n. 261.

97 'Östlicher und westlicher Kommunismus', *Proletarier*, no. 1 (October 1920); Gorter, *Offener Brief an den Genossen Lenin . . ., passim*; and Gorter, 'Partei, Klasse und Masse' (1921), op. cit.

98 'Lehren der März-Aktion', *Proletarier*, no. 5 (April–May 1921); [A. Pannekoek], 'Sowjetrussland und der westeuropäische Kommunismus', op. cit. (June 1921). Cf. also Pannekoek's letter to Erich Mühsam (at the end of 1920), in which he declared his wholehearted solidarity with the Bolsheviks (cited by Bricianer, op. cit., pp. 215–17).

99 'Bericht über Moskau', *Die Aktion*, nos 39–40 (September 1920).

100 'Die russische Staatspolitik und ihre Konsequenzen für die Kommunistische Internationale', *Proletarier*, no. 6 (June 1922); 'Thesen über Moskau', *Rätekorrespondenz*, no. 3 (August 1934); *Von bürgerlichen zur proletarischen Revolution*, op. cit., ch. 2, 'Das russische Problem'.

101 *Workers' Councils*, section ii, ch. 5, 'The Russian Revolution'.

102 Cf. *The New World*, pamphlet published by the 'Groups of Council Communists Holland' (Amsterdam 1947), and A. Pannekoek, *Workers' Councils*, final section, 'The Peace', as well as his article 'The Failure of the Working Class', *Politics*, vol. 3 no. 8 (September 1946), cited by Bricianer, op. cit., pp. 283ff.

103 Symptomatic is the chapter on the workers' councils (written by an ex-KAPist, Paul Mattick) published in an anthology claiming to be representative of the New Left: P. Long (ed.), *The New Left* (Boston, 1969). On the councillist tradition in France since the Second World War, cf. my *Les origines du gauchisme* (Paris, 1971), ch. 4 (English translation: *The Origins of Modern Leftism*, Penguin Books, 1975).

104 The thesis of the 'fatal crisis of capitalism' was current in councillist
circles in the 1930s. This theme was
taken up again in the 1940s, and
Pannekoek still speaks of a gradual
worsening of capitalism's positions
in his *Workers' Councils*, pp. 225–7.

See also Mattick's essay on workers'
councils (op. cit. in n. 103).
105 'The Workers' Councils', *International Council Correspondence*, op.
cit.
106 Rühle, *Von bürgerlichen zur proletarischen Revolution*, op. cit., p. 51.

4 The critique of Marxian reification

1 In line with recent usage, I shall use
the adjective *Marxian* to indicate
what refers to Marx himself; *Marxist*
will therefore refer to his doctrine as
a whole, as interpreted by his disciples.
2 After the Second World War, Jorn
played a part in the International of
Experimental Artists, which published   the   review   *Cobra*
(Copenhagen–Brussels–Amsterdam).
He helped found the Internationale
Situationniste in 1957, leaving it in
1961. His *Critique de la politique
économique* was published in the
'Rapports présentés à l'Internationale Situationniste' series in
1960.
3 G. Lukács, *Geschichte und Klassen-
bewusstsein* (1923).
4 The paragraph is entitled 'The two
factors of a commodity: use-value
and exchange value or value proper'.
5 'When, at the beginning of this
chapter, we said, in common par-
lance, that a commodity is both a
use-value and an exchange value,
we were, accurately speaking,
wrong. A commodity is a use-value
or object of utility, and a value.' *Capital*, ch. 1, section 3, A, 4: 'The
elementary form of value considered as a whole' (translated by S.
Moore and E. Aveling, edited by F.
Engels, London, 1889).
6 Jorn points out that, from the point
of view of its theoretical foundations, *Capital* is inseparable from the
so-called philosophical works of
Marx's   youth.   Philosophically
speaking, the origins of this identification lie in the ill-conceived relationship between subject and
object. In his *1844 Manuscripts*
(which Marx himself described as a
'necessary settling of accounts between criticism and its origins – i.e.
Hegelian dialectics') Marx develops

a Kantian conception of the noume-
non and the phenomenon, and fails
to see the movement, the dialectic
that makes alienation (*Entfremdung*
or *Entäusserung*) the process
whereby the self objectivizes. As a
result Marx's conception of the in-
itself and of the for-itself is a static
one; they are seen as an opposition,
within thought itself, between abstract thought and sensible reality
('Der Gegensatz des abstrakten
Denkens und . . . der sinnlichen
Wirklichkeit . . . innerhalb des
Gedankens selbst'). Marx adds that
all oppositions are merely the
exoteric form of this fundamental   opposition   (*Ökonomisch-
philosophische Manuskripte*, 3rd MS,
p. xvii). Most 'Marxologists' have
now   abandoned   the   Hegelian
descendance thesis. The Feuer-
bachian origins of Marxian thought
are attested to by 'bourgeois science'
(cf. D. McLellan, *The Young
Hegelians and Karl Marx*, London,
1962, pp. 101ff) and by 'communist
science': ('For us, the question from
where did Marx arise? is therefore of
the highest importance: he arose
from neo-Hegelianism, which was a
returning-back from Hegel to Kant
and Fichte, and then from pure
Feuerbachism. . . .' (L. Althusser,
'Avertissement' to Book I of *Capital*,
Paris, 1969).
7 Marx (*Capital*, pt 1, ch. 1) reduces
the capital formation process to the
exchange of commodities, whereas
it implies first the manufacture of
the object of utility and its non-
utilization straightaway.
8 Two banknotes of the same face-
value are indistinguishable apart
from their serial numbers.
9 'When viewed, therefore, as a con-
nected whole, and as flowing on
with incessant renewal, every social
process of production is, at the same

time, a process of reproduction.' (Quoted by Jorn from *Capital*, pt 1, ch. 23.) And also, 'The conditions of production are also those of reproduction' (ibid., Moore-Aveling translation).

10 We are dealing with private saving here: economically, the socialist revolution (or communist revolution – according to Jorn the two are distinguishable not in terms of their goals but in terms of the 'means of acceding to power') is embodied in the abolition of private saving. Right from the outset, saving will be social, i.e. forced.

11 Lenin· successively held each of these two views. In *State and Revolution* (Petrograd, 1918) he begins by calling for the destruction of the State, and refers to Marx in doing so. But Marx's 'anarchism' concerns the higher phase: communism. Jorn seems unaware of the fact that, for the transition period, Marx calls for a dictatorial State: on this point, there is no difference between the young Marx and the mature Marx. ·Cf. his letter to Weydemeyer, 5 March 1852, in which he states that the class struggle necessarily leads to the dictatorship of the proletariat (letter cited by Lenin in the 2nd edn of his pamphlet in support of his thesis concerning the proletarian State). Some 20 years later, in his *Marginal Notes on the Programme of the German Workers' Party* (1875) he once more re-stated that, in a period of political transition, the State 'could not be anything other than the *revolutionary dictatorship of the proletariat*'.

Bibliography

Where translations into English are cited, references are usually to most recent editions or impressions or to those most likely to be accessible. A number of works in this bibliography were issued without information about the date and/or place of publication.

ANWEILER, O., *The Soviets: The Russian Workers', Peasants', and Soldiers' Councils (1905–1921)* (tr. from German), New York, 1975.

ARSHINOV, P., *History of the Makhnovist Movement (1918–1921)* (tr. from Russian), Detroit/Chicago, 1974.

AVRICH, P., *Kronstadt 1921*, Princeton, 1970.

AVRICH, P., *The Russian Anarchists*, Princeton, 1967.

AVRICH, P., *The Russian Revolution and the Factory Committees*, Ann Arbor (University Microfilms), 1973.

BAKUNIN, M., *Selected Writings*, London, 1973.

BAKUNIN, M., *Statism and Anarchy*, New York, 1974.

BAKOUNINE (Bakunin), M., *Oeuvres*, Paris, 1890–1911.

BERKMAN, A., *The 'Anti-Climax'*, Berlin, 1925.

BERKMAN, A., *Die Kronstadt Rebellion*, Berlin, 1923.

BERKMAN, A., (ed.), *The Russian Revolution and the Communist Party*, Berlin, 1922.

BOCK, H. M., *Syndikalismus und Linkskommunismus von 1918–1923*, Meisenheim am Glan, 1969.

BORCHARD, J. *Revolutionshoffnungen* (brochure), Berlin, 1917.

BRICIANER, S., *Pannekoek et les conseils ouvriers*, Paris, 1969.

BRINTON, M., *The Bolsheviks and Workers' Control*, 1970.

BROUÉ, P., *Révolution en Allemagne (1917–1923)*, Paris, 1971.

BRUPBACHER, F., *Marx und Bakunin*, Munich, 1922; Berlin, 1969.

BURNHAM, J., *The Managerial Revolution*, Penguin Books, 1962.

CAMMETT, J. M., *Antonio Gramsci and the Origins of Italian Communism*, Stanford, 1967.

CARDAN, P., *From Bolshevism to the Bureaucracy*, London.

CARDAN, P., *Modern Capitalism and Revolution*.

CARDAN, P., *Socialism or Barbarism*.

CARR, E. H., *The Romantic Exiles*, Penguin Books, 1949.

CARSTEN, F. L., *Revolution in Central Europe (1918–1919)*, London, 1972.

CASTORIADIS, C. [Pierre Chaulieu], *La société bureaucratique*, Paris, 1973.

CHATELET, F., *Hegel*, Paris, 1968.

CIESZKOWSKI, A. VON, *Prolégomènes à l'historiographie*, Paris, 1973.

COLE, G. D. H., and POSTGATE, R., *The Common People*, London, 1968.

COLE, G. D. H., *Guild Socialism*, London, 1920

COQUART, A., *Dmitri Pisarev (1840–1868) et l'idéologie du nihilisme russe*, Paris, 1946.

DANIELS, R. V., *The Conscience of the Revolution*, Cambridge, Mass., 1960.

DUNAYEVSKAYA, R., *Marxism and Freedom*, London, 1971.

ENGELS, F., *Ludwig Feuerbach and the Outcome of Classical German Philosophy*, New York, 1941.

ENGELS, F., *Socialism: Utopian and Scientific*, London, 1972.

ESTIVALS, R., *L'avant-garde culturelle parisienne depuis 1945*, Paris, n.d. [1962].

FABBRI, L., *Dittatura e rivoluzione*, 1921.

FAURE, S. (ed.), *Encyclopédie anarchiste*, Paris, 1924 (*The Anarchist Encyclopedia* (tr.), vol. 1, New York, 1974).

FISCHER, G., *Russian Liberalism*, Cambridge, Mass., 1958.

FLECHTHEIM, O. K., *Die K.P.D. in der weimarer Republik*, Frankfurt, 1969.

FOOTMAN, D., *Civil War in Russia*, London, 1961

FREYMOND, J. (ed.), *La première internationale* (2 vols), Geneva, 1962.

GAVRONSKY, D., *Le bilan du bolchévisme russe*, Paris, 1920.

GOLDMAN, E., *The Crushing of the Russian Revolution*, London.

GOLDMAN, E., *My Disillusionment in Russia*, New York, 1923 (many later editions).

GOLDMANN, L., *Recherches dialectiques*, Paris, 1959

GOMBIN, R., *The Origins of Modern Leftism* (tr. from French), Penguin Books, 1975.

GORTER, H., *Die Klassenkampf-Organisation des Proletariats*, Berlin, 1921 (repr. in Pannekoek, A. and Gorter, H., *Organisation und Taktik der proletarischen Revolution*, Frankfurt, 1966).

GORTER, H., *Offener Brief an den Genossen Lenin, eine Antwort auf Lenins Broschüre: Der Radikalismus, eine Kinderkrankheit des Kommunismus*, Berlin, n.d. [1921].

GORTER, H., *Réponse à Lénine*, Paris, 1930.

GRAMSCI, A., *L'Ordine nuovo*, 1955.

GRUNBERGER, R., *Red Rising in Bavaria*, Bristol, 1973.

GUÉRIN, D., *Rosa Luxemburg et la spontanéité révolutionnaire*, Paris, 1971.

HEGEL, G. W. F., *Hegel's Science of Logic*, London, 1969.

HEGEL, G. W. F., *Lectures on the History of Philosophy* (3 vols), London, 1956.

HEGEL, G. W. F., *Reason in History* (partial tr.), New York, 1963.

HERZEN, A., *Du développement des idées en Russie*, London, 1853 (repr. in French, New York, 1974).

HERZEN, A., *From the Other Shore*, London, 1856.

HERZEN, A., *Lettres de France et d'Italie*, Geneva, 1871 (repr. in French, New York, 1974).

HERZEN, A., *Le monde russe et la révolution*, Paris, 1860–2 (repr. in French, New York, 1974).

HERZEN, A., *My Past and Thoughts* (4 vols), London, 1968.

HORNER, K. [A. Pannekoek], *Sozialdemokratie und Kommunismus*, Hamburg, n.d. [1919].

Internationale Situationniste (1958–69), Amsterdam, 1970.

JAY, M., *The Dialectical Imagination*, London, 1973.

JORN, A., *Critique de la politique économique*, Paris, n.d. (1960).

KAUFMANN, W. (ed.), *Existentialism from Dostoevsky to Sartre*, New York, 1956.

KEEP, J. L. H., *The Rise of Social Democracy in Russia*, Oxford, 1963.

KOLB, E., *Die Arbeiterräte in der deutschen Innenpolitik 1918–1919*, Düsseldorf, 1962.

KOLLONTAI, A., *Workers' Opposition, 1919–20*.

KOOL, F. (ed.), *Die Linke gegen die Parteiherrschaft*, Olten, 1970.

KUBANIN, M., *Mahnovščina*, Leningrad.

LABRY, R., *Alexandre Ivanovic Herzen*, Paris, 1928.

LABRY, R., *Herzen et Proudhon*, Paris, 1928.

LAMPERT, E., *Studies in Rebellion*, London, 1957.

LEHNING [Müller], A., *Anarchisme et marxisme dans la révolution russe*, Paris, 1971.

LEMKE, M. K. (ed.), *Polnoe sobrane sočinenij i pisem* (22 vols), Petrograd, 1915–25.

LENIN, V. I., *The Development of Capitalism in Russia*, London, 1957.

LENIN, V. I., *Left-wing Communism: An Infantile Disorder* (1920), New York, 1965.

LENIN, V. I., *One Step Forward, Two Steps Back* (1904), London, 1969.

LENIN, V. I., *State and Revolution* (1918), London, 1972.

LICHTHEIM, G., *Lukács*, London, 1970.

LIEBKNECHT, K., *Politische Aufzeichnungen aus seinem Nachlass*, Berlin, 1921.

LIEBMAN, M., *Leninism under Lenin* (tr. from French), London, 1975.

LONG, P. (ed.), *The New Left*, Boston, Mass., 1969.

LOZINSKIJ, E. I., *Čto že takoe, nakonec, intelligencija?*, St Petersburg, 1907.

LUKAĆS, G., *History and Class Consciousness: Studies in Marxist Dialectics* (tr. from German), London, 1975.

LUXEMBURG, R., *The Mass Strike, the Political Party and the Trade Union*, Detroit.

LUXEMBURG, R., *The Russian Revolution*, Ann Arbor, 1961.

LUXEMBURG, R., *Selected Political Writings*, London, 1972.

MCLELLAN, D., *The Young Hegelians and Karl Marx*, London, 1969.

MACHAJSKI, W., *Buržuaznaja revolucija i rabočoe delo* (1905); *Bilans buržuazyjnej rewolucyi rosyjskiej* (Geneva, 1909); *La faillite du socialisme au XIXème siècle* (manuscript): all in the Max Nomad Foundation, International Institute for Social History, Amsterdam.

MAKHNO, N., *La révolution russe en Ukraine*, Paris, 1970.

MALIA, M., *Alexander Herzen and the Birth of Russian Socialism*, Cambridge, Mass., 1961.

Manifestes, thèses et résolutions des quatre premiers congrès mondiaux de l'Internationale communiste, Paris, 1968.

MARX, K., *Capital*, many editions.

MARX, K., *The Civil War in France*, New York.

MARX, K., *Critique of Hegel's 'Philosophy of Right'*, Cambridge, 1970.

MARX, K., *Critique of Political Economy*, London, 1971.
MARX, K., *Economic and Philosophic Manuscripts of 1844*, London, 1970.
MARX, K., *The Eighteenth Brumaire of Louis Bonaparte*, New York, 1963.
MARX, K., *The Grundrisse: The Foundations of the Critique of Political Economy*, Penguin Books, 1973.
MARX, K., *La question juive*, Paris, 1968.
MARX, K. and ENGELS, F., *Critique des programmes socialistes*, Paris, 1948.
MARX, K., and ENGELS, F., *German Ideology*, New York, 1970.
MARX, K. and ENGELS, F., *Collected Works*, London, from 1975, in progress.
MASINI, P. C., *Antonio Gramsci e l'Ordine nuovo. Visti da un libertario*, 1956.
Massenaktion, Berlin, 1933.
MAURICIUS, *Au pays des soviets*, Paris, n.d. [1921].
MAXIMOFF, G. P., *Syndicalists in the Russian Revolution*, London.
MEHRING, F., *Karl Marx, The Story of His Life* (tr. from German), London, 1936.
MÉSZÁROS, I., *Lukács' Concept of Dialectic*, London, 1972.
METT, I., *Kronstadt Commune*, 1967.
NOMAD, M., *Aspects of Revolt*, New York, 1961.
NOVOMIRSKIJ, *Čto takoe anarhizm*, n.p. (Geneva), 1907.
OERTZEN, P. VON, *Betriebsräte in der Novemberrevolution*, Düsseldorf, 1962.
ORGEIANI, K. [G. Gogelija], *Ob intelligencii*, London, 1912.
PANKRATOVA, A., *Fabzavkomy Rossij v borbie za socialisticheskuju fabriku*, Moscow, 1923.
PANNEKOEK, A., *Die taktische Differenzen in der Arbeiterbewegung*, Hamburg, 1909.
PANNEKOEK, A., *Weltrevolution und kommunistiche Taktik*, Vienna, 1920.
PANNEKOEK, A., *Workers' Councils*, Melbourne, 1950.
PANNEKOEK, A. and GORTER, H., *Organisation und Taktik der proletarischen Revolution*, Frankfurt, 1969.
PASCAL, P., *Les grands courants de la pensée russe contemporaine*, Lausanne, 1971.
PASCAL, P., *La révolte de Pougatchev*, Paris, 1971.
PAYNE, R. (ed.), *The Unknown Karl Marx*, London, 1972.
PESTAÑA, A., *Informe de mi estancia en la URSS*, Madrid, 1968.
PIOTTE, J. M., *La pensée politique de Gramsci*, Paris, 1970.
PORTAL, R., *Slavs* (tr. from French), New York, 1970.

PRIBICEVIC, B., *The Shop Stewards' Movement and Workers' Control*, Oxford, 1959.

Programm der kommunistichen Arbeiter-Partei Deutschlands, n.d. [1920].

PROUTEAU, H., *Les occupations d'usines en France et en Italie (1920–1936)*, Paris, 1937, 1967.

R[IZZI], B., *La bureaucratisation du monde*, n.d. [1939].

ROCKER, R., *Der Bankrott des russischen Staatskommunismus*, 1921.

ROCKER, R., *Les soviets trahis par les bolchéviques*, Paris, 1973.

RÜHLE, O., *From the Bourgeois to the Proletarian Revolution* (tr. from German), 1974.

RÜHLE, O., *Die Revolution ist keine Parteisache!*, Berlin, 1920.

SADOUL, J., *Notes sur la révolution bolchévique*, Paris, 1919, 1971.

SCHMOLZE, G., (ed.), *Revolution und Räterepublik in München 1918–1919 in Augenzeugenberichten*, Düsseldorf, 1969.

SCHORSKE, C. E., *German Social Democracy (1905–1917)*, Cambridge, Mass., 1955.

SCHRÖDER, K., *Vom werden der neuen Gesellschaft*, Berlin, n.d. [1920].

SCHWARZ, A., *Die weimarer Republik*, Konstanz, 1958.

SERGE, V., *Memoirs of a Revolutionary* (tr. from French), London, 1967.

SHATZ, M. S., *Anti-intellectualism in the Russian Intelligentsia*, Certificate of Russian Institute, City University of New York, 1963 (mimeo.).

SIMMONS, E. J. (ed.), *Continuity and Change in Russian and Soviet Thought*, Cambridge, Mass., 1955.

SOUCHY, A., *Wie lebt der Arbeiter und der Bauer in Russland und in der Ukraine*, Berlin, n.d. [1920?].

SOURINE, G., *Le fouriérisme en Russie*, Paris, 1936.

STIRNER, M., *Ego and His Own* (tr. from German), London, 1971.

STUART HUGHES, H., *Consciousness and Society*, London, 1959.

TASCA, A., *The Rise of Italian Fascism, 1918–1922* (tr. from Italian), New York.

TAYLOR, C., *Hegel*, Cambridge, 1975.

TOKÉS, R. L., *Béla Kun and the Hungarian Soviet Republic*, New York, 1967.

TROTSKY, L., *In Defence of Marxism*, London, 1966.

TROTSKY, L., *Nos tâches politiques*, Paris, 1971.

TROTSKY, L., *Rapport de la délégation sibérienne*, Paris, 1970.

TROTSKY, L., *The Revolution Betrayed*, London, 1973.

TROTSKY, L., *Terrorism and Communism*, London, 1975.

VADÉE, M., L'idéologie, Paris, 1973.

VANEIGEM, R., Traité de savoir-vivre à l'usage des jeunes générations, Paris, 1967.

VENTURI, F., Roots of Revolution: A History of the Populist and Socialist Movements in Nineteenth Century Russia, New York, 1966.

VÖLGYES, F., The Hungarian Soviet Republic, Stanford, 1970.

VOLINE, Le fascisme rouge, Brussels, n.d. [1931].

VOLINE, Nineteen-Seventeen, London, 1954.

VOLINE. The Unknown Revolution, London, 1955; Detroit/ Chicago, 1974.

VOLSKIJ, A. (Machajski), Umstvennyj rabočij, Geneva, 1904–6; New York, 1968.

WOLFFHEIM, F., Betriebsorganisationen oder Gewerkschaften, Hamburg, 1919.

YVON, M., Ce qu'est devenu la révolution russe, Brochure de la Revue Prolétarienne no. 2, n.d. (1936).

Index

A A U D *see* General Workers' Union of Germany
Alexander II, Assassination of, 59
All-Russian Workers' Control Council, 20
anarchism
Bakunin's influence on, 63; Bolshevik adoption of programme of, 34–5; council communists tendency towards, 113; critique of Bolshevism by, 32, 33–9; as 'destructive passion', 6; as heir to Herzen's socialism, 54; Marxist aversion for, 6, 33; rejection of, by Machajski, 69; rise in response to capitalism, 70
anarcho-syndicalist union, FAU, 101
anarcho-syndicalists in Germany, 36, 101; in Russia, 37
anti-authoritarianism, 11–12, 45
Antonov, A. S., leader of social revolutionaries, 27
April Theses (Lenin), 36
Arshinov, Peter, Ukrainian leader, 25
art, avant-garde, challenge to orthodox Marxism, 120
artistic revolution, of Jorn, 124–5

autonomy, in workers organizations, 83, 89
as central for councillists, 118
Avrich, Paul, historian of Russian anarchism, 36
Axelrod, P., social democrat, 71
criticisms of RSDWP by, 72, 74, 80; 'help' for workers' strikes, 79

Babouvism, critique of, by Herzen, 59, 62
Bakunin, M., 6, 54, 59
critique of Marxism, 38, 52, 63–5; followers of, excluded from Second International, 33; influenced by Hegel, 46; Machajski influenced by, 69
Bauhaus, in Weimar Germany, 120
Belinsky, V. G., 54, 56
influenced by Hegel, 46
Bernstein, Edward, and revisionist right of German Socialist Party, 94
'biological economy' as result of Marxist economics, 123
Blanc, Louis, 53, 62
and organization of labour, 48, 57; as theoretician of state socialism, 62

Bolsheviks
    agrarian programme of, 17, 36; ascen-
    dancy of dogma of, 10; centralization
    of power by, 27–8; control of trade
    unions by, 21; criticism of, 32–43; and
    dictatorship of proletariat, 12; ideolog-
    ical principles and conquest of power
    by, 17–18, 27–30, 34–8, 73; Kronstadt
    sailors hatred of, 31; relationships
    with soviets, 14–16; resistance to,
    23–7, 31–2; split with Mensheviks, 73,
    80; and workers' control, 18–22
Borchardt, Julian, council communist,
    113
Bordiga, Amadeo, followers of, 39
bourgeoisie
    absence of, in Russia, 50; and capita-
    lism, 66; culture controlled by, 7, 112;
    new, 11; and nineteenth-century
    revolutions, 54; relations with pro-
    letariat, 4–8; and Russian Revolution,
    74, 77, 115; values imposed on pro-
    letariat, 7; workers struggle with, 7,
    68
Breshnovskaya, 'little grandmother of
    the revolution', 35
Brest-Litovsk, Treaty of (1918), 24, 115
    as end to anarchist hopes, 36
bureaucratic class
    as beneficiaries of socialism, 4; pro-
    ductivist views of, 5; in Soviet State,
    40–3
bureaucratic collectivism, 41

Capital, Das, Jorn's critique of, 120–1
capitalism
    bureaucratic, in USSR, 42; destruc-
    tion of, as aim of AAUD, 101; evolu-
    tion of, 7–8; Herzen's view of, 53; and
    increase in petit bourgeoisie, 66;
    orthodox communism like, 11, 41–3;
    and rise of anarchism, 70; socialization
    of consumption by, 124
class consciousness of proletariat
    raising of, 111, 112–13; and revolu-
    tions, 95, 105
class dictatorship, 77, 108
collectivization of land, 17, 27, 115
commodities
    in Marxist thought, 121–2; production
    by capitalism, 124; relationship to
    objects of utility, 123
commodity cycles, 122
communism
    changed recruitment to, 11–12; party,
    106, 109   see also council communism
Communist International, Comintern
    (Third International) and KAPO, 103,
    104; dissident Marxist break with, 39;
    and Marxism–Leninism, 5, 10; party

communism of, 103, 107; Second
    Congress of (1920), 105
Communist Manifesto, 63
Communist Workers' International,
    KAI, 106, 110
Communist Workers' Union, 102
Comte, Auguste, French philosopher, 2,
    3
consumer societies, 8
consumption, socialization of, 124
council communism, 81–118
    break with Comintern, 39; as opposed
    to party communism, 106, 109; prob-
    lems of organization and, 109–114; on
    Russian Revolution, 114–16; theory of,
    101–2, 106–9, 117–18
councillist party, temptation to form, 110
Critique de la politique économique (Jorn),
    120
culture
    bourgeois control of, 7, 112; as 'con-
    sumer good', 8

dignity of man, Herzen's insistence on,
    51–2
Dutch Marxists, 95–6, 107
Dutch Social Democratic Party, SDAP,
    110, 111

'economists' within Russian Marxists,
    68, 71, 79
education
    limited nature of proletariat, 7; Mach-
    ajski's belief in, 68
Eisner, Kert, Bavarian republic pro-
    claimed by, 86
Engels, Friedrich
    Marxism a cosmogony, 3; as theoreti-
    cian of state socialism, 62
Erfurt Congress (1891) of German Social-
    ist Party, 93

factory committees
    in Germany (Betriebsorganisationen),
    100–1; in Russia (fabzavkomii), 18–21, 37
factory occupations, 81
    in Italy, 90; after World War II, 116
FAU see anarcho-syndicalist union
FAUD see German Free Workers' Union
federalism, advocated by Herzen, 52
feminism, Herzen's support of, 48, 52
Fourier, François, French social theorist
    influence on Russian socialists of, 2,
    47, 48; mistrust of French Revolution,
    62
Fourth International, of Essen tendency
    of KAPD, 103, 106
Fourth International, of Trotsky, 39
Franco-Russian war, and opposition to
    Tsars, 46

Frankfurt school, and Marxist philosophy, 119
Free Russian Press, influence of, 51
French Revolution
bourgeois nature of, 74–5; and radical theory, 2; as source of Russian Jacobinism, 62

General Workers' Union of Germany, AAUD, 101, 102–3
German Communist Party, KPD
formation of, 99; merger with USPD, 100; size of, 107; split in, 99–100, 104
German Free Workers' Union, FAUD, 101
German General Workers' League – Unitary Organization, AAUD-E, 102, 111
German Social Democrat Party, SPD
in Bavaria, 86; collaboration with Imperial government of, 84–6; left-wing opposition inside, 93–4
German Workers' Communist Party, KAPD, 100, 104
centrifugal tendencies of, 102–3; leaders of, 110; refused by Second Congress of Comintern, 105
'Go to the People' movement, 58, 79
Goldman, Emma
The Truth about the Bolsheviki, 35
Gorky, Maxim, on soviets, 16
Gorter, Herman, Dutch poet, 105–6, 117
and proletarian organizations, 110–11
Gramsci, Antonio, and workers' councils, 90–2
Greater Berlin Workers' and Soldiers' Council, 84, 85
Guild Socialists, in England, 88

Halberstadt, Congress of (1892), 93
Hegel, Georg William Friedrich, 121
influence on Russian socialists, 46–7
Heidelberg Congress (1919), 100, 104
Herzen, Alexander Ivanovich, 39
dislike of bourgeois ideologies, 53–4; influences on, 46–9; popularization of socialism in Russia by, 46–7; radical principles of, 51–3; socialism of, 54–7
Humanità Nuova and criticism of Bolsheviks, 35
Hungarian Soviet Republic, 86

intellectual capital, nature of, 66
intelligentsia
Bakunin's critique of, as new aristocracy, 63–4; bourgeois nature of, 64; *déclassé* intellectuals, 61; as leaders of proletarian revolution, 58–60, 66–7, 77–8; monopoly of knowledge of, 69; political struggles within, 71, 79–80;

professional, 61; rise of, in nineteenth-century Russia, 55–6; RSDWP run by, 74–5; Western, 55
International Communists of Germany, IKD, 99
International Socialists, ISD, 107
Internationals, group of German left-wing radicals, 99
IKD formed by, 99; Russian Revolution welcomed by, 103
Iskra, 71–2
Italian Socialist Party, PSI, 90
IWW American union-based revolutionary organization, 102

Jacobinism
Leninism as, 77; populism moving towards, 55; Russian, 58, 60, 62
Jogiches, assassination of, 104
Jorn, Asger, Danish painter and philosopher
artistic revolution of, 124–5; criticism of Marxist philosophy by, 120–4; definition of reification by, 121; theory of form of, 122

KAPD *see* German Workers' Communist Party
Kater, Fritz, German independent socialist, 93
Kautsky, Karl, and 'Marxist Centre' of German SPD, 94
passive attitude of, 96; theories of, 95
Korsch, Marxist philosopher, 119
KPD *see* German Communist Party
Kronstadt rising, 22, 23, 30–2, 36
demands of, 30–1
Kropotkin, Prince Peter, followers of excluded from Second International, 33
Kun, Béla, Hungarian leader, 87–8

labour, militarization of, 22, 28–9
land
collectivization of, 17, 27, 34, 115; distribution of, 25, 26; nationalization of, 25
Landauer, Gustav, German independent socialist, 93
Lavrov, Peter, and young activists, 59
left-wing radicals in Germany, 93, 94, 97
extremist groups of, 98; opposition to war of, 98; Spartakus group in, 98–100
Lenin, Vladimir Ilyich
and Bolshevik seizure of power, 33, 36; compared to Robespierre, 75; control of RSDWP by, 72–3; letter of, to left-wing German communists, 104–5; NEP introduced by, 27, 115; organizational utopia of, 74–5, 79; on soviets, 15; and workers' control, 20, 21

Leon, Daniel de, American socialist, 91
Levi, Paul, and right-wing of KPD, 99, 101, 104
Léviné, Eugene, Bavarian communist leader, 86
libertarians, Russian
concerned with problems of action, 70; Machajski's rejection of, 69; opposition to Bolshevik regime of, 37
Liebknecht, Karl
assassination of, 104; on right-wing of KPD; 99; and Spartakus group, 98
Lozovsky, Russian trade unionist, 21
Lukaćs, Georg, Marxist philosopher, 119
reification defined by, 121
Luxembourg, Rosa
assassination of, 104; criticism of social democratic movement by, 72, 76–8, 80; leader of German left-wing radicals, 94–5; on right-wing of KPD, 99; and Spartakus group, 98

Machajski, Jan Waclaw, 43, 45
on economic struggle of proletariat, 68–9; on importance of strikes, 68–9; socialism as ideology of intelligentsia, 65–8, 80
Makhno, Nestor, Ukrainian leader, 23
death of, 26; peasant soviets and unions formed by, 24; persecution of, by Bolsheviks, 25–6
Makhnovshchina
military significance of, 23; political resistance of, 23–6
Martinov, social democrat Marxist, 71
Marx, Karl
confusion of value and object by, 121; economism and, 4–5, 120; as philosopher, 119–120; reification by, 121; on savings, 123, 124; as scientist, 2–3, 120; on status of proletariat, 5, 6, 67; as theoretician of state socialism, 62; and theory of form, 122
Marxism
Bakunin's critique of, 69; centralizing and authoritarian potential of, 64–5; debt to anti-authoritarian socialism, 69; divided, in Russia in 1890s, 71; and economism, 4–5, 120; ideology of, 3–5; intelligentsia and, 67, 79–80; as scientific system, 2–3, 120–1; state capitalism as aim of, 5–6, 17; Trotsky's views on, 28
Marxism–Leninism, 106
developed by intelligentsia, 45; as dogma of Bolsheviks, 10
mass action, proletariat need for, 107
mass spontaneity, Pannekoek's theory of, 111–13, 116

Mass Strike, the Political Party and the Trade Union, The (Luxemburg), 76, 94
Mehring, Franz, and Spartakus group, 98
Mensheviks
split with Bolsheviks, 73, 80; tactics of, 73; and workers' management, 17, 19
metalworkers' federation in Italy, FIOM, 90–1
metalworkers' strikes, 88, 90
middle-class, mercantile, 6
lack of, in Russia, 56
miners' strikes in England, 88
Minor, Robert, Bolsheviks criticized by, 35
money, as socialized commodity, 123
monogamy, Fourier's attack on, 48
Movement for an Imaginist Bauhaus, 120
munitions industry, strikes and unrest in, 88
mutinies, naval, in Germany, 85

National Conference of the Shop Stewards' Movement, 89
nationalization, 22, 25, 115
Nechaev, revolutionary, 58, 63
New Economic Policy, NEP, 27, 115
Nihilists, tenets of, 58
Novomirski, and intelligentsia's monopoly of knowledge, 69

Odessa Committee, 75
Ogarev
editor of Kolokol, 51; influence of Hegel on, 46–7
organization in workers' parties, 94, 99, 104
'Our Political Tasks' (Trotsky), 75
Owen, Robert, influence of, 51

palingenesis, as social regeneration, 47
Pan-German Congress of Councils, 84, 85
Pankratova, A., Soviet historian, 20
Pannekoek, Anton, astronomer and Dutch left-wing leader, 95, 110
criticism of 'Marxist Centre' by, 95–6, 103; editor of Vorbote, 103; and Internationalist Group, 99; and KAPD, 100; production as essence of society, 117; on Russian Revolution, 115–16; theory of mass spontaneity, 111–13, 116
Parliamentarianism
council communists view of, 106–7; KPD divergence on, 99, 104; Lenin's support for, 105; socialism not reached by, 95–6

peasants
as beneficiaries of revolution rather
than workers, 58; ignorance of, 59;
lack of response of, 59
Peterson, V. B., Dane
Symboler i abstrakt Kunst, 120
Petrashevsky, and Fourier's doctrines,
48
Petrograd Central Council of Factory
Committees, 20, 22
Petrograd Soviet, 14, 15
Phenomenology of Mind, The (Hegel), 121
Plekhanov, Georgi Valentovich, social
democrat, 71, 72
'help' for workers' strikes, 79
populism in Russia, 45
defeat of, 60; derived from Herzen's
socialism, 54, 57, 79; evolution
towards Jacobinism, 55, 60; as source
of anarchism and social democracy, 33
Potressov, social democrat Marxist, 72
Profintern, First Congress of the Red
International of Trade unions, 36
proletariat
dictatorship of, 67, 99, 101; economic
struggle of, 68–9, 71; education as
saviour of, 68; leaders of revolution of,
77–8; mass action by, 106–7; myth of
support for Russian Revolution,
22–32; organizations of, 81, 106; political development of, 6–7; relations with
bourgeoisie and bureaucratic class,
4–8, 41–2; urban, in Russia, 60
property, private, and NEP, 115
Proudhon, Pierre-Joseph, and Russian
socialists, 48–9

Radek, Karl, and right-wing of KPD, 99,
104
Radischev
Journey from Saint Petersburg to Moscow,
46
reification in Marxist philosophies,
121–4
revolutions
and bourgeoisie, 54, 74, 77, 115; and
communist parties, 11; failure of
1848–9 European, 4; in history of Russia, 49–50; proletarian, 108, AAU–E as
organization of, 111
see also French Revolution, Russian
Revolution
Ricardo, David, on status of proletariat, 6
Rizzi, Bruno, and bureaucratic class, 41
Rocker, Rudolf, German anarchist, 101
Roland-Holst, H., social democrat, 95,
103
Rühle, Otto
and AAUD–E, 102, 111; demy-
thologizing of Russian Revolution,

115; and KAPD, 105, 111; 'revolutionary party' as nonsense, 107, 111;
and Spartakus group, 98
Russian Revolution
as bourgeois, 106, 115; councillist
views of, 114–16; as dictatorship of
party rather than class, 114; defeat for
radicality, 10; and Internationals, 99;
myths of, 12–39; and radical socialists,
103; solidarity with, 35; and soviets,
12–16, 81
Russian Social Democratic Workers'
Party, RSDWP
bourgeois nature of, 74–5; condemned
by Rosa Luxemburg, 77; Congress of
(1903), 72; hierarchical and centralized
nature of, 73; programmes of, 15, 34

Saint-Simonism, 2, 3, 47
saving, and surplus, 123–4
Schröder, Karl
'Essen' tendency of KAPD formed by,
103; visit to Moscow of, 105
science
Herzen's dislike of, 54; intelligentsia
influenced by, 64; Marxism and, 2–3,
120; Tchernishevsky's confidence in,
57
SDAP *see* Dutch Social Democratic
Party
Second International
Bolshevik role in, 103; Dutch break
with, 95, 96; Spartakist links with, 99
Second International Anarchist Congress (1921), 35
self-management and workers' control,
16–22
serfdom, abolition of, 49
Shidlovski Commission, 13
shop-floor delegates, committees of, 81
shop-stewards' movement, 88–9, 91
social capital, and savings, 123
social change
by using state machine, 59; 1914–21,
82–3
social democracy
and anarchism, 70; criticism from
within, 76–8; essence of, in RSDWP,
73; as ideology of intelligentsia, 45
Social Democratic Party of Holland,
SDP, 95, 110
Social Democratic Workers' Party of Holland, SDAPH, 95
social democrats in Russian Marxism,
71, 79–80
split into Bolsheviks and Mensheviks,
80
Social Democrats' Congress (1903), 72
social revolutionaries, 34
and revolt against Bolsheviks, 26–7

socialism
  anti-authoritarian tradition of, 8–9;
  aristocratic, 55–7; beneficiaries of,
  4; as concentrated capitalism, 42–3;
  development of, in Russia, 45–61; as
  ideology of intelligentsia, 65–8, 80;
  road to, via Statism, 28–9; scaling
  down of, seen by Machajski, 67–8;
  trend towards, 4
Socialisme ou Barbarie, 41–3
Socialist Labour Party of England, 88
Souchy, A., German anarcho-
  syndicalist, 36
Soviet state, 10–43
  attitudes towards, 39–43; critique of,
  11–12; Marxism as official ideology of,
  5; myths of, 12–32
soviets
  Bolshevik control of, 14–16; as myth of
  Soviet state, 12–16; as puppets, 36;
  and Russian Revolution, 81; types of,
  12–14
Spartakus group, 98–100
SPD *see* German Social Democrat Party
Stalinism, 40
  anti-authoritarian socialism eliminated by, 8–9
State capitalism
  aim of Marxism, 5–6; as equal to state
  socialism, 115
State and Revolution (Lenin), 19, 27, 34,
  103
Statism, as road to socialism, 28–9
strikes
  in Germany in World War I, 84, 97; in
  Hungary in World War I, 87; important for workers, 68–9; in Italy after
  World War I, 90; in Lodz, 68; in Petrograd, 30; and shop-stewards' movement, 88–9
  see also wildcat strikes

Tambov, rising, 26–7
Tchernishevsky
  capitalism criticized by, 49; and state
  intervention, 57
terrorism, rise of, 58–9
thoery of form, 122
Tkachev, theoretician or Russian Jacobinism, 58, 62, 63
Toller, Ernst, Bavarian soviet leader,
  86
trade unions
  capitalist nature of, 95–6, 97; conflict
  with working class of, 107; and councillist theory, 106, 116; 'entryism' and,
  104, 105; and FAUD, 101; German
  left-wing criticism of, 93; Gramsci's
  views on, 91–2; Russian, controlled by
  Bolsheviks, 21, as purely educational,

30, and workers' control, 20–2; and
  shop-stewards' movement, 88–9
Trades Union Congress, workers' control adopted by, 88
Tribunists, Dutch, 94, 95
Troelstra, P. J., Dutch Marxist, 95
Trotsky, Lev Davidovich, 28–32
  criticism of social democratic movement by, 72, 75–6, 80; excluded from
  power, 39–40; and Kronstadt rising,
  31–2; and Makhnovshchina, 25; and
  militarization of labour, 22, 29–30;
  Soviet state as transition regime, 43
Trotskyists
  break with Comintern, 39; Soviet state
  criticized by, 39–43
Tsars, 59
  opposition to, and Franco-Russian
  war, 46

Unitary Workers' League, AAU–E, 111,
  113
USPD, independent social democrat
  party, 85
  in Bavaria, 86; foundation of, 98;
  merger with KPD of, 100

Vico, Giovanni Battista
  Scienza Nuova, 1
villages
  assemblies (*skhod*), 14; autonomous
  peasant (*mir*), 50–1, 52
Volontà, Italian anarchist journal, 35
Vorbote, 103

'War Communism', 26–7
What is to be Done (Lenin), 71, 72, 111
White Russians, and Makhnovshchina,
  23, 25
wildcat strikes, 81, 82, 84, 89
  as new form of conflict after World
  War II, 116
work, in councillist theory, 117
workers' conspiracy, of Machajski, 68–9
workers' control, 88
  history of, in Russia, 16–22
workers' councils
  in Austria, 83–4; in Bavaria, 86; and
  communism, 92; dictatorship of proletariat through, 109; in England, 88–9;
  in Germany, 84–6; in Hungary, 86–8;
  in Italy, 90–2; management of production by, 109; and proletarian revolution, 108–9
Workers' Group, 70
Workers' Opposition, 22
Workers' Soviet of Budapest, 87
Workers' Truth, 70
World War I, and workers' struggle,
  83–9

World War II, 40, 116
    and council theory, 116; and criticism
    of Soviet State, 40

'Young People' of German Socialist
    party, 93

'Young Russia' group, 57
Yvon, M., hostility to Stalinism, 40

Zasulich, V., social democrat, 71
    assassination of, 72; Trepov shot by,
    59